MW01505473

BEREAVEMENT AND FINAL *SAMSKĀRA* (*ANTYEṢṬI*) IN HINDU TRADITION

By

SRI DHIRA CHAITANYA

ISBN # 0-9777008-1-X

Published by: Sri Dhira Chaitanya

First Edition: 2005
Reprint: 2007

Books are available from the following:

Amazon.com and other retailers

http://www.purnavidya.com

Chennai, India
Purna Vidya Trust
"Mamtha" Basement
8A, 2nd street, North Gopalapuram
Chennai 600086
Tel: (0)44-28352573

TABLE OF CONTENTS

Message from Pujya Sri Swami Dayananda 04
Author's Note 05

PSYCHOLOGICAL INSIGHTS 08
Attitudes toward Death and Dying 08
Coping with the Final Moments 16
Solace from Hindu Traditions 19
Process of Bereavement 37

ANTYEṢṬI SAMSKĀRA 42
Introduction 42
Cremation Ceremonies 49
Ceremonies During Mourning Period 59
Ceremonies after Mourning Period 67
Śrāddha Ceremony 68
Unusual Circumstances of Death 78

VEDIC INSIGHTS 82
Introduction 82
Scientific and Religious Thought 83
The Law of *Karma* 86
Karma, Birth and Rebirth 89
Life after Death 99
Īśvara 103
Dharma, the Universal Moral Order 106
Understanding *Mokṣa* 111
Jīvanmukti 116

MESSAGE FROM PUJYA SRI SWAMI DAYANANDA

Bereavement is grief for every human being. This is so because the departed individual is not going to be around in the same form any more in the entire future. This creates a void in the connected ones leaving them to ruminate over the past omissions and commissions in regards to the departed.

Even though people think that time helps one to cope with grief, it is not true. Time never heals. In time we heal ourselves by resorting to different methods. But all of them don't work to one's satisfaction. Hindu Tradition over the ages has followed certain prayerful religious practices as well as varieties of psychological means to assimilate the reality of death. Even in life the reality of death is objectively faced in Hindu Culture. All these facts are presented in detail in this book by Sri Dhira Chaitanya.

As a practicing Psychiatrist in New York, he has helped a lot of people to cope with bereavement, and also as a Hindu Religious leader in the community, he has been helping the bereaved in the community religiously as well. This two fold experience makes him the right person to write a book of this kind which will definitely help one understand and assimilate the reality of death.

Swami Dayananda Saraswati

AUTHOR'S NOTE

In my professional capacity as a Child Psychiatrist, I have had numerous occasions to work with patients, children and adults, who were terminally ill and dying. I have also worked with children, who were struggling to cope with the death of a parent or a family member. In my role as a religious teacher, I have been called upon countless times, under a wide variety of circumstances to respond to the needs of the members of the Hindu community, in dealing with the death of their family members. Neither of the above prepared me adequately for dealing with my personal feelings at the demise of my father and subsequently my mother. It was only when I experienced the death of my parents and was required to perform all the elaborate religious rituals that I gained an appreciation of the profoundness of Hindu religious rites, traditions and customs connected to the death of an individual.One cannot but be impressed by the depth of insight of our ancestors, into the nature of the human mind and it's functioning. The fact that the ceremonies associated with the funeral and the traditional mourning period have sustained basically unchanged for thousands of years only highlights the fact that they serve a meaningful purpose. The final *saṃskāra (antyeṣṭi)*, when performed with understanding and sincerity, undoubtedly help an individual connected to the deceased, go through the bereavement process and emerge from it, as a more mature individual. Thereby, the bereavement process also becomes a spiritually uplifting one.

It is unfortunate and somewhat disheartening to observe that, in current times, there appears to be a decline in value among many Hindus, for performing final *saṃskāra* for their loved ones who are no more. Perhaps, it is due to a lack of understanding of the meaning and significance of Hindu religious traditions and customs. Or perhaps, the pressures of modern times rob an individual of the inner leisure, to experience, deal with, overcome and grow from their emotions, even when they are painful and difficult. It is with the hope of filling this gap in understanding that I undertook to write this book at the suggestion of my teacher and guide Pujya Sri Swami Dayananda Saraswati.

I take this opportunity to thank some significant people whose assistance was invaluable to me. I am grateful to the priests Shri Sharmaji, Ganeshan and Ravi whose sensitivity and thoroughness in helping me perform *saṃskāra* for my parents gave me invaluable insight into Hindu traditions. I thank Swamini Pramananda for her invaluable insights and help in editing and Usha Ramaswamy, for her ongoing support, insights and assistance with editing. I thank Nirmala Shankar, Sri Ramakrishnan and his team at Sastraprakasika Trust for their support in publication of this book.

I would like the reader to note that while I am sensitive to avoiding gender bias, I have generally made use of the male pronoun in the text. This is only to prevent awkwardness in reading.

I humbly offer this work of mine at the feet of my Guru, Pujya Sri Swami Dayananda Saraswati who has been my teacher, guide, and a beacon of light in my lifelong journey. To him I owe all my insights, values and immeasurable wealth of knowledge of my rich traditions and heritage.

I dedicate this book to the memory of my father, Shri Ramaswamy and my mother Giani, who in their demise taught me many lessons, just as they did so lovingly in life.

Sri Dhira Chaitanya

1

PSYCHOLOGICAL INSIGHTS
ATTITUDES TOWARD DEATH AND DYING

Emotional Reactions:

A person deals with one's own impending death in a variety of ways. The kinds of responses that one has are influenced by one's culture, beliefs, personal values and personality. Upon becoming aware of one's impending death, it is natural and quite common to become anxious. Every individual cherishes his life. So, the real likelihood of its coming to an end is an unwelcome thought that one does not want to entertain. Often a person's initial reaction is one of denial. The anxiety in such a person's mind does not permit him to accept the reality and inevitability of his own impending death. There is an apprehension in talking about death or dying, expressing one's feelings, planning for the well being of one's family and taking care of one's personal affairs.

Initially the person talks and behaves as if everything is as usual. Denial is not a conscious, deliberate decision not to talk. It is an unconscious protective mechanism of the mind to cope with a highly anxiety provoking situation at a particular time. The period of denial may be transient or remain with the person until his death. Denial may at times lead to a feeling of invulnerability, even leading to reckless behavior.

Sometimes a person does not deny the inevitable but avoids dealing with it directly. This is done in order to protect himself or others from the unpleasant and difficult emotions associated with death. Such a person may preoccupy himself with mundane matters that are unconnected with the fact of his death and thereby spare himself and others the agony of painful feelings. Fear is another common emotion experienced by a dying person. The possibility of impending death evokes a fear of the unknown.

No one knows for sure, what would happen after one's death. The continuity of one's very existence is put to question. And, no one is ready to die to find the answer. Additionally, there is the fear of loss of one's family and friends. These are the people who have been the source of support in one's life and have helped one deal with many difficult situations in the past. However in this particular instance, when death is at one's doorstep, they are as helpless as oneself in doing anything to prevent it. Often, there is illness associated with dying which gives rise to fear of pain and suffering. Quite often, one has ideas of the process of death that are dramatic and frightening, because one may have witnessed a traumatic death, or have been influenced by what one sees in the media.

An individual who is aware of his impending death often experiences sadness. He worries, his sleep gets disturbed and he may lose his appetite. He is unable to enjoy anything pleasant. He may cry and appear morose. Any experience of loss or the possibility of loss evokes sadness in an individual, even when it is the loss of oneself due to death. To begin with, there is the concern that one would cease to exist and thus be lost forever.

Even if one were to continue, it certainly would not be in the current shape and form, as one has to necessarily give up one's body at the time of it's death. Whatever complaints one may have about one's body, it is the only one that one has had and is familiar with. The thought of losing it forever naturally evokes sadness. Besides experiencing sadness, one may go through a process of mourning for the impending loss of oneself, much the same as one goes through bereavement process after any loss. Sometimes, one can become melancholic and withdrawn to the extent that one isolates oneself from one's own loved ones emotionally and/or physically. Individuals may also experience guilt in varying degrees. One starts recalling a lifetime of acts of omission and commission. In retrospect, one realizes that there is much that one would like to have done, and maybe much more that one could have avoided doing. This is not only in regards to one's personal pursuits, but also in one's relationships with others. Knowingly or unknowingly, one invariably becomes instrumental in causing hurt in another individual, either by one's action or by one's words. No individual wants to maliciously and deliberately hurt someone he is related to. Thus, one experiences guilt and given a chance would like to make amends for all the hurt that one may have caused. Guilt can cause considerable fear in an individual who has grown up to believe in the prospect being punished after death for eternity, with varieties of horrible experiences for not conforming to prescribed codes and dogmas.

Anger is another common emotion experienced by the individual facing immanent death. Anger arises when one perceives oneself as a victim of an act of injustice that one has been subject to. It also arises when one feels helpless in a given situation.

Even though death is an inevitable fact of life, it is also true that one does not willingly accept its occurrence. Moreover, a significant part of ones time is devoted to maintaining one's life and extending it as long as one possibly can. Even if one acknowledges that death is bound to occur one day, the timing of it's arrival always seems premature. One wonders, "why am I the chosen one at this time, I am not ready to die, to leave my loved ones" and so on. These thoughts make one feel helpless and give rise to anger. Sometimes, sadness is also expressed as anger. Thus we find that a person facing impending death becomes irritable, easily angered and may even unreasonably blame others such as family, friends, doctors and sometimes even God for what is happening to him or her.

In conclusion, some individuals are more accepting of the inevitability of death than others. Even though they feel a certain degree of sadness for various reasons such as loss of their loved ones, they have essentially reconciled to the fact that they are dying. They can articulate their thoughts, feelings, and fears, seek and gain comfort and support from those around them. Their beliefs and traditions provide them with strength, reassurance and comfort. For one who ascribes to Hindu traditions, one's beliefs and the basis of the Hindu religious and cultural traditions become a source of strength, reassurance and comfort. Hindu tradition emphasizes that the occurrence of birth underscores the certainty of death at some point.

जातस्य वै मनुष्यस्य ध्रुवं मरणमिति विजानीयात् ।

jātasya vai manuṣyasya dhruvaṃ maraṇamiti vijāneeyāt

Know that for the individual who is born, death is inevitable indeed.

The Vedic tradition places a certain value on dispassion, *vairāgya*, in regards to the world and the people one encounters in one's life. This attitude is based on an understanding of the ephemeral nature of the whole universe. *vairāgya* is not viewed as a fatalistic attitude that impairs one from functioning in the world and relating to it appropriately. It is an appreciation of the truth of it's nature, which in fact makes one relate to the world as it is. It permits one to make the most of one's association with the world and the people one spends one's life with. The following verse highlights the attitude of *vairāgya* the transient nature of the world:

गृहेष्वर्था निवर्तन्ते श्मशाने चैव बान्धवाः ।
शरीरं काष्ठामादत्ते पापं पुण्यं सह वृजेत् ॥

gṛheṣvarthā nivartante śmaśāne caiva bāndhavāḥ
śarīraṃ kāṣṭhamādaṭṭe pāpaṃ puṇyam saha vṛjet

One's possessions are left behind at home and relatives (left behind) on the cremation grounds.
The body is consumed in the funeral pyre; only ***Purṇyaṃ*** *and pāpaṃ accompany (one).*

Vedic tradition also enquires into the ontological status of the world of experiences, and the relationship between oneself, the universe and it's cause. An understanding of these matters helps an individual deal with not only himself and others, but also with life and death.

Bertrand Russell eloquently described death as a concluding episode of one's life and an integral part of existence. Using a metaphor he said that an individual's existence should be like a river – small at first, narrowly contained within its banks, and rushing passionately past boulders and over waterfalls. Gradually, as the river grows wider the banks recede, the water flows more quietly and in the end, without any visible break, it becomes merged in the sea and painlessly loses its individual form.

Reactions in Family Members:

The ones who are close to a dying person also have to deal with a variety of emotions of their own. They too get anxious about what is happening around them. They may be engaged in the medical and nursing care of the person that can be tiring and overwhelming, not to mention confusing. They feel a profound sense of helplessness because of their inability to prevent what is happening to their loved one. They feel that they are letting him down.

Their profound sense of helplessness sometimes evokes anger at others for not doing more than what they are doing. This anger can get directed towards other caretakers, such as doctors, nurses or other family members. It can result in petty misunderstandings between family members that in turn, evoke guilt as one feels embarrassed at one's own reactions. Anger can also get directed towards God, who is seen as being responsible for causing them pain and not responding to their prayers to spare the one they love.

They experience fear of losing someone they love and perhaps rely upon. The possibility of never again being able to see and live with a loved one evokes both fear and sadness. They begin to imagine what it would be like to live without their loved one.

Ruminating over the future is the way a person's mind tries to prepare itself for an undesirable experience that it anticipates and fears.

Families also feel pressured to maintain an appearance of normalcy in front of their dying member. They are afraid that if they reveal how upset they are, the person may not be capable of handling their distress. Thus, they avoid showing their feelings, which does not really serve any purpose, as people who are close to each other can usually sense each other's unexpressed feelings. Thus, their attempt at protecting one another in this manner does not usually work.

There is no ideal way which would be universally applicable, in order to cope with the difficult situation of impending death in a family. Every individual affected by it, deals with it in the way he know best and in the manner in which his mind is comfortable and capable. However, one can say that, in general, it is advisable to be as communicative as one possibly can. When a person does not know what another thinks, they start guessing what might be in the other's mind. Very often what they imagine is not only inaccurate, but also exaggerated and worse than it is. Additionally, it is generally easier to deal with something that one knows than with the unknown. This is so even with respect to dealing with another person's thoughts and feelings. Protecting one another in a difficult situation that involves death, only compounds one's sense of helplessness as one is unable to change what is happening and also unable to prevent other's agony. Sharing one's thoughts, feelings, concerns, fears and so on, is comforting, even though it may be difficult to do.

People discover a tremendous amount of strength from each other during difficult times. When faced alone, a difficult situation looks impossible to overcome. However, a seemingly impossible situation becomes manageable when endured along with people one trusts.

Conclusion:

In relating to individuals facing death, it is best to remain one's natural self. It is not necessary to act as if nothing is happening. Doing so, only gives a message that one does not wish to deal with the difficult issue at hand. It prevents the dying individuals from expressing their wishes, and sharing their feelings. It places an added burden on them to deal with death alone and leaves them feeling unsupported. By encouraging them to express themselves to the extent they are comfortable, one can provide them with a lot of support. One needs to make them feel that they have someone, who though incapable of changing the inevitable, is willing to be by their side until the very final moment of their lives.

In order to help a loved one who is facing immanent death, it may become necessary to put aside for a while one's own sadness and feeling of deprivation at one's impending loss. During such a difficult time one's religious traditions and beliefs become a source of strength and comfort, for both the dying and those closely connected to him or her.

2

COPING WITH THE FINAL MOMENTS

There are occasions of impending death, when both the dying person and those connected to him know that death is inevitable and immanent. There is a fear of the unknown. There is fear of annihilation. And, there is fear of losing all one is familiar with. One may be overcome by a sense of helplessness. There is also sorrow at separation from all that one is attached to and one loves. Very often, those that one is connected to are also very sad.

Both the dying person and his family try to protect each other, and may pretend that everything is as usual and fine. It is very difficult to suggest how one should behave during these times. People tend to do what is most comfortable to them and what may be appropriate in case of one family may not be so in case of another. When one is able to, it is very helpful to share one's thoughts and feelings with those one is close to. To talk to a loved one about one's feelings and fears is very comforting to both. Even if what one speaks causes sadness, when sorrow is shared with a person one loves, it is easier to experience.

It is a rare gift to be able to express oneself and share one's thoughts and feelings with one's loved one who is dying. This is so because, very often death comes unexpectedly, or a dying person may be incapacitated or in pain. It is a very common experience for people, to feel that they did not say what they would have liked to say to a person who is no more, and they live with this sense of incompleteness for the rest of their lives. It is in such difficult times that one's religious convictions and spirituality become a source of great solace.
Generally, Hindus recite verses from the Vedas such as *Kṛṣṇa Puruṣasūktaṃ Bhagavad Geetā Rāmāyaṇa*, and *Viṣṇusahasranamam*. It is believed that what one's mind is attuned to at the time of death, determines one's gati, direction of onward journey after death and also one's next birth. Therefore, the family and friends of a dying person provide an environment of spirituality and comfort during the final moments of his or her life.

In *Bhagavadgītā*, (Chapter 8, Verse 5) Lord *Kṛṣṇa* assures Arjuna the following:

अन्तकाले च मामेव स्मरन्मुक्त्वा कलेवरम् ।
यः प्रयाति स मद्भावं याति नास्त्यत्र संशयः ॥८.५॥

antakāle ca māmeva smaran muktvā kalevaram
yaḥ prayāti sa madbhāvaṃ yāti nāstyatra saṃśayaḥ

The one who gives up his body remembering me (the Lord) during his final moments reaches me. Of this there is no doubt.

Unless a person has lived prayerful life it is difficult for him to remember the Lord during his final moments. People everywhere have their own beliefs about what happens to an individual after death. But there is no one, who has seen a dead person come back to report to those alive about their experience, in a manner that can be verified by them with certainty. There are however, innumerable cases investigated, reports documented and available that have been verified indirectly to a greater or lesser degree about after death experiences and reincarnation. Most people do accept that there is an entity in addition to the physical body that survives death and remains in some form. However, not knowing for certain makes the unknown future frightening.

There is also a sadness that comes from the knowledge that one will never again see those that one loves and has spent one's life with. Moreover, no one can take with them any of the possessions that they have accumulated in their lifetime and have to leave behind all that they are attached to. There can also be a fear of possible pain and suffering associated with the process of death itself.

3

SOLACE FROM HINDU TRADITIONS

Religious traditions provide meaning to a human being's life and his very existence. In the Vedic tradition, important life events are marked by religious ceremonies called *saṃskāras*, sacraments and include the *antyeṣṭi saṃskāras*, the sacrament performed upon the death of an individual.

For a person who looks at the world in non religious terms, to deal with the death of a person involves disposing of the decomposing corpse of the deceased, managing his estate and getting over the feelings generated by the loss of the deceased. For an individual who lives a religious life, with an appreciation of the Lord, dealing with death of an individual he is connected to, while being essentially a sad experience also becomes a spiritually uplifting one.

To deal with one's irretrievable loss and experience the multitude of emotions associated with it, within the framework of religious tradition and beliefs, make it possible for one to cope with a very difficult experience, and come out of it as a more sensitive and mature individual.

Solace Before Death Occurs:

Religious traditions, one's beliefs and understanding offer solace even prior to one's demise. There are times when a person is cognisant of his impending death. A person aware of the end of his life in this world, naturally feels that he would like to settle all his accounts with the world before he departs from it. If one has time and is inclined to, one may perform acts of atonement, *prāyaṣcitta* karmas, in the form of giving charity *dānam*. Religious codes of conduct, *dharmaśāstra*, advise charity in the form of gifting a cow, *godānam*. The cow given in charity is called *vaitaraṇee* or *anustaraṇee* one that helps a person cross over (the boundary between life and death). A person can perform this charity himself or the cow is given later as a part of the *antyeṣṭi* ceremonies after his death.

A person preparing for death may feel that there are things that he wanted to do that are not done, or things he wanted to say to significant others that are unsaid. He may want to be relieved of a sense of guilt at acts of commission and omission that he feels responsible for. Sometimes one deals with these feelings by making direct or indirect contact with significant people in one's life. One likes to have one's family around, to bid farewell to them.

One's family and friends also like to be present to give support and bid farewell. The family prays individually and together, seeking strength from the Lord to help them cope with what they are going through. When a person is aware of his impending death he tries to engage his mind in remembering the Lord by reciting his name and thinking of his glories. Those around him facilitate this by reciting verses from the Vedas, the *Bhagavadgītā Rāmāyaṇa Viṣṇusahasranama* and so on. This serves to comfort the dying person and also those around him. It is believed that when an individual utters the name of the Lord and constantly remembers him, after the death of his physical body he reaches the abode of the Lord, from where he does not return to a life of sorrow and limitation

मृतो विष्णुपरं याति न पुनर्जायते श्रृतौ
सकृदुच्चारितं येन हरिरित्यक्षरद्वयम् ।
बद्धः परिकरस्तेन मोक्षाय गमनं प्रति
कृष्ण कृष्णेति कृष्णेति यो मां स्मरति नित्यशः ॥

Mṛto viṣṇuparaṃ yāti na punarjāyate śṛtau
SakṛduccāritaM yena hariritakṣaradvayam
Baddhaḥ parikarastena mokṣāya gamanaṃ prati
Kṛṣṇa kṛṣṇeti kṛṣneti yo māṃ smarati nityaśaḥ

One who chants the two-syllable name Hari, goes to the heavenly abode of the all pervasive Lord.
The one who constantly remembers me repeating my name Kṛṣṇa kṛṣṇa, is freed from bondage and goes towards mokṣa.

In other words, dwelling upon spiritual matters makes a jiva's future more favorable spiritually, besides giving him comfort at the present time.

In the *Bhagavadgītā* (8.6), Lord *Kṛṣṇa* explains to Arjuna the lot of a person who is nearing death in the following verse:

यं यं वापि स्मरन्भावं त्यजत्यन्ते कलेवरम् ।
तं तमेवैति कौन्तेय सदा तद्भावभावितः ॥८.६॥

yaṃ yaṃ vāpi smaranbhāvaṃ tyajatyante kalevaram
taṃ tamevaiti kaunteya sadā Tadbhāvabhāvitaḥ Kṛṣṇa

O Arjuna, thinking of whatever object a person gives up the body at the time of death, that very object (he) attains, being constantly absorbed in that thought.

More specifically Lord *Kṛṣṇa* points out that if a person engages his mind in thinking of the Lord at the time of his death he attains the ultimate abode of the Lord. This belief is quite prevalent among the Hindus. Therefore people try to create a spiritual environment around a dying person and typically, if given a choice a Hindu would like his final moments to be such that he is being comforted by his faith while he breathes his last. Whenever possible, holy water, *tīrthaṃ* from sacred rivers such as *Gangā* is given to the person. If the person is unable to ingest it, the family will place a few drops of it in the mouth symbolically as a purificatory act of after death.

4

SOLACE AFTER DEATH HAS TAKEN PLACE

The religious traditions associated with the death ceremonies can be understood at different levels. They may be understood as a religious mandate based purely on *śhraddhā*, faith based on reason and trust, and as a time tested means of helping a human being experience an inevitable and undesired fact of life, namely death, in a meaningful manner. The traditions can also be understood by appreciation of the scripture as a means of knowledge for things that are beyond the scope of human intellect. We will take a look at each of these aspects.

The Vedas are looked upon as a means of knowledge in regards to matters that are beyond the scope of knowledge of a human mind to arrive at by itself. A human mind can gain knowledge of various matters directly by sense perception and indirectly by inference based on sense perception. An average person cannot directly perceive what happens to an individual after his death.
That the Vedas are a means to know the unknown, naturally leads one to the question about the validity of the Vedas as a means of such knowledge. Many religious traditions establish the authenticity of their scripture by calling upon the faith of an individual to unquestioningly accept what they say. Vedic tradition establishes the authenticity of the Vedas in a manner indicated below:

The Vedas talk about various ends and the means to accomplish them. In the pursuit of means and ends, there can be known means for achieving known ends, unknown means for achieving known ends and unknown means for achieving unknown ends. Clearly, one cannot have known means for achieving unknown ends. In the first case, the known means for achieving known ends are available to man, for instance how to reach a given destination. In the second case, there are desired ends for which either the means are unknown or the means that are known to accomplish the given end do not achieve their purpose due to unknown factors that are beyond human control.

In this instance the Vedas provide the means in the form of specific karmas, rituals that address the unknown factors. For example, the Vedas provide a specific ritual called *purtrakāmeṣṭī yāga* for one who desires to have a son and is unable to do so due to reasons beyond human control. Another example of how the Vedas serve as an unknown means for a known end is by providing the means for self-knowledge, knowing the essential nature of Oneself. In this case the self, subject is available but its essential nature is unknown because it cannot objectify itself. By understanding the words of the Vedas one is able to gain self-knowledge. In the third case, the Vedas identify unknown ends such as heaven and the unseen results of karma *adṛṣṭam*, in the form of merit, *puṇyam*, and demerit, *pāpam*, with respect to the moral order, Dharma.

Vedas also provide us the means to reaching heaven and the means of modifying the results of karma by doing specific acts of atonement, *prāyaścitta* karmas.

One can verify the authenticity of the Vedas as a means of knowledge by operating the means given to accomplish ends that are known. These ends are achievable in one's lifetime.

Individuals, who do the karmas as prescribed by the Vedas, find that they do bear the results they are meant to. With respect to self-knowledge, tradition has established the truth of the words of the Vedas as a means of knowing oneself. Self-knowledge has been passed down from one generation to the next, in an unbroken line of teaching tradition to the present day, and is available for any individual to access. The Vedic tradition also emphasizes that what is said in the scripture should be consistent with reason and not contradicted by experience.

One thus develops trust in the words of the Vedas as a means of knowledge, in regard to unknown ends and the means for achieving them, since what they say is not illogical and is not contradicted by experience.

Psychological Benefit from Post-death Religious Ceremonies:

The *Antyeṣṭi*, funeral and the ceremonies performed during the period of mourning address both the deceased and the bereaved family. The ceremonies are based on the Vedic vision of the individual and his relationship with *Īśvara*, Lord and the universe.

The life of a Hindu is a spiritual one and his culture religious. From birth to death, his life is lived with the appreciation of oneness with Isvara Moreover, the entire universe is seen as a manifestation of Isvara and thus non-separate from him. A

Hindu's life is also guided by an understanding of the universal order of Dharma and Adharma and the laws of karma. He believes that a person's existence does not begin with birth and terminate with death of the physical body. There is an indweller of the body called jiva prana who manifests in a given body

in order to experience the results of it's prior karmas. When a given physical body has served it's purpose, deteriorates and is unable to sustain life the jiva gives up its current form to assume another more suitable one to continue its experiences based on the results of prior karmas.

After death of an individual, the immediate concern of his family is for the proper disposal of the dead body. Among the Hindus, preparation of the body for disposal is not left to professionals who are unconnected to the deceased. The family prepares the body for cremation and stays with it until it is cremated. This makes the whole experience of losing a loved one very intimate and intense. While it is undoubtedly difficult to deal with one's sadness and myriad of emotions and at the same time do what needs to be done, it makes one experience the consequences of death at very close quarters. It makes a person see the reality of death and the impermanence of life, in a manner that is vivid and unforgettable. Most individuals avoid thinking of such matters while engaged in their average day to day activities. In appreciating the reality of death, one learns to value life clearly and not take it for granted.

Several regional customs such as tying the toes of the corpse together, tying a cloth around the jaws and so on are meant to prevent the undesirable effects of rigor mortis on the dead body.

The religious ceremonies performed prior to cremation are meant for the disposal of the dead body with sanctity, reverence and care. In addition, they provide a healing touch to the bereaved family. By the ceremonies the body is sanctified and made fit for cremation from a religious perspective, *dahanayogya*.

Ritual purification is performed by a process of anointing the body with water that has been made holy by chanting mantras and offering prayers and oblations to various deities. In the Hindu tradition, the southern direction represents mortality and death and so the body is placed with its head towards the south. The recitation of scripture such as the *Bhagavadgeetā* (chapter 8), and selected verses from *Kaṭhopaniṣad*(chapter1) and *Iśāvāsyopaniṣad* (verses 15-18) provide comfort and give a message to the bereaved and the departed, as these verses deal with what happens to an individual after death.

Hindus believe that the deceased had a deep identification with his physical body in order to experience the world. He also had a reciprocal attachment to his family, and an attachment to his possessions. As such he is expected to have difficulty in transitioning from the known physical to a subtle world that is unknown and new to him. Of course, at this time the family also has difficulty accepting the reality of his death. Just as one "assumes" a dream body that is intangible in order to experience the dream world, so also a jiva is believed to assume a subtle body after death of the physical body, in order to experience the results of the karmas performed by it. Immediately after death this subtle form is referred to as preta. The preta is a transitory form that exists for a period of time in which the deceased maintains some connections with the world he has known. The bereaved family also maintains a connection with the deceased during the period that immediately follows his demise. They do this through the ceremonies associated with the cremation and the mourning period of thirteen days. The ceremonies provide a form to the sentiments that are both known and unknown. In this manner, the ceremonies help the process of separation for both the deceased and the bereaved by reminding them that the formers time in his recent earthly form is over and his connections with the world that he has left behind have come to an end. He needs to continue and move on in accordance with his karmas.

From the time of death until the end of the cremation it is customary for the extended family and friends to be present. They assist the immediate family in various procedures and provide support. After the body of the deceased is placed on the pyre, the final ceremonies associated with cremation are performed. They include purification of the cremation site and the body, and invocation of the Lord. Ghee is poured on the pyre as an offering to Lord Agni before and during the cremation. Scripture and tradition have established ghee as an offering for Lord Agni. Ghee serves as a fuel and is thus an appropriate offering unto fire. And unlike petroleum ghee is also a food item. Thus it becomes an ideal offering to appease the Lord invoked in the form of Agni.

In one of the significant and poignant steps during the cremation ceremony, the person about to light the pyre on which the body of the deceased is placed, goes around it three times reciting the following verse:

ओं कृत्वा तु पुष्करं कर्म जानत वाप्यजानतं
मृत्युः कालवशं प्राप्य नरं पञ्चत्वमागतम् ।
धर्माधर्म समायुक्तं लोभमोहसमावृतं
देहेऽयं सर्वगोत्राणि दिव्यान् लोकान् स गच्छतु

oṃ kṛtvā tu puṣkaraṃ karma jānata vāpyajānatam
mṛtyuḥ kālavaśaṃ prāpya naraṃ pañcatvamāgataṃ
dharmādharma samāyuktaṃ lobhamohasamāvṛtaṃ
deheyaṃ sarvagotraṇi divyān lokān sa gacchatu

Having performed known and unknown actions for attaining prosperity; having gained timely death and resolved the physical body into the five elements, having concluded a life of desires and connected to Dharma *and* Adharma, *may you proceed to heavenly abode.*

Such verses encapsulate the sentiments and beliefs of a Hindu. They also become a source of strength, to perform some very difficult tasks that are associated with the experience of losing a loved one to death.

After cremation of the body, the family and friends leave the cremation grounds and take a purificatory bath before returning home. At this time the members of the immediate family, *bandhus*, offer water oblations to the departed by facing towards the south. They also offer prayers to Lord invoked as *Prajāpati*. They sit around for a while, talking about the deceased and about the transitory nature of life and the world.
Pondering over these matters and sharing their thoughts and feelings with each otherhelps them cope with their loss.

When they return to their homes, before entering the house it is customary to step on a stone seeking strength from the Lord with the following prayer:

अश्मनिव स्थिरो भूयासम् ।

*aśmaniva sthirō bhūyā***sam**

May I remain firm and unshaken as this stone.

The bereaved observe religious impurity, *aśaucam*, as will be explained later.

The ceremonies performed during the initial period of grieving last for thirteen days. During this time, the bereaved family forsakes all pleasures and observes behavior that is indicative of grief and mourning. They sleep on the floor and deny themselves comforts and luxuries. This is very much in keeping with their state of mind during this period. During bereavement one is unable to enjoy anything pleasurable. Any attempt at feeling good makes one feel guilty. The bereaved spend their time talking about the departed and their loss. The hearth is kept unlit in the home of the bereaved until the cremation ceremonies are completed. This is because fire has to be lit only as ritual fire at this time, for the purpose of offering unto it the body of the deceased. During the bereavement period other family members and friends provide the bereaved with food.

Family and friends also visit them in order to offer them their condolences. The bereaved repeatedly talk about the deceased, their feelings and their loss. They share their sorrow with each other. Such reminiscing helps them ease the pain of their loss and go through the process of bereavement. Bereavement process involves learning to accept one's loss, allowing oneself to experience the feelings associated with it such as sadness, guilt, helplessness, anger and so on, and being able to eventually resume one's normal life.

During the customary mourning period the bereaved family goes through rather intense experiences. The rituals give form to sentiments that one may or may not be conscious of. The physical acts of invoking the deceased, imagining his presence, relating to him and interacting with him in the form of making offerings, all help to evoke emotions in the bereaved that may be difficult to experience and accept ordinarily. The support the bereaved receive from family and friends who take care of them and share their sorrow, makes their sadness easier to bear. The repeated prayers to the Lord in various forms give them strength. Performing acts of atonement for the deceased in the form of giving charity to those in need helps them overcome to an extent their feelings of helplessness and guilt.

Tenth to Thirteenth Days:

The ceremonies of the tenth, eleventh and twelfth days are elaborate and important. On the tenth day the deceased is invoked in it's *preta* form and offered food. The bereaved family makes special efforts to prepare food items which were liked by the deceased. The family prays to Lord Yama, the presiding deity of death and dharma, to end the *preta* state of the deceased and to bless it so it may proceed on it's journey. Lord *Vāyu* is also invoked with the following prayer and implored to bless the deceased:

अनादिनिधनो देव शङ्खचक्रगदाधर
अक्षय्य पुण्डरीकाक्ष प्रेत मोक्षप्रदो भव ॥

anādinidhano dēva śaṅkacakragadādhara
akṣayya puṇdarīkākṣa pretamokṣaprado bhava

O Effulgent lotus-eyed one, who is without beginning, not subject to declining, holding the conch, discus and mace, please release (the jiva) from its preta *form.*

Feeding is a universal expression of love and caring. When the bereaved make a special effort to prepare food and offer it to one they have lost by invoking his presence, it gives them an opportunity to express their love and caring to the person. Needless to say, the food offering is symbolic and not expected to be physically eaten by the deceased. However, one cannot minimize the importance and usefulness of form to express the sentiments that are associated with it.

One normally experiences some degree of guilt upon the death of someone that one is close to. It is quite normal to think of all one could have said and done and was unable to do, if only one had any inkling that the person would die. Some of the ceremonies do help the bereaved overcome their feelings of guilt and sense of incompleteness in this regard. Do the offerings really reach the deceased? The Vedas assure us that they do, of course not literally in their physical form but in their subtle form as a result of the karma performed by the family.

The following verse explains:

यदाहारा भवान्त्येते पितरो यत्र योनिषु
तासु तासु तदाहाराः श्राद्धानेनोपतिष्ठति ।
यथा गोषु शनश्तासु वत्सो विन्दति मातरं
तथान्नं न याते विप्रो जन्तुर्यत्रावतिष्ठते ॥

yadāhārā bhavāntyete pitaro yatra yoniṣu
tāsu tāsu tadāhārāḥ śrāddhānenopatiṣṭhati
yathā goṣu śanaśtāsu vatso vindati mātaraṃ
tathānnaṃ nayate vipro janturyatrāvatiṣṭhate

Whatever is offered to ancestors during Shraddha ceremony goes to them in whichever form they exist.
Just as a calf finds its mother among the scattered herd.

The ceremonies of the eleventh day incluae prayers for the release of the Jiva from the transient form of preta. Prayers to Lord *Vāyu*, the sustainer of the universe ask for the Jiva's continued wellbeing. *Dakṣina* is given to *Brahmaṇas* who are also invited for a meal. Gods and ancestors are invoked in the *Brahmaṇas* who by virtue of living a religious life of discipline are considered suitable recipients, *mahāpātra*, for this honor.On the twelfth day the concluding ceremonies connected to the *preta* are performed.

The main ceremony is called *sapiṇḍikaraṇaṃ*, which means union of the Jiva with its ancestors, pitrs After this day the deceased is no longer referred to as *preta*.

The family does not pray for the welfare of the deceased, but prays to him as an ancestor for his blessings for their own well-being. This day brings about a shift is the attitude of the family towards the deceased. They gain a degree of objectivity and distance emotionally from the deceased, look upto him with gratitude and offer worship. In some religious traditions the body of the deceased is kept for a few days before being disposed of. This gives people connected to the deceased an opportunity to say their farewell, and come to terms with the physical absence of the deceased over a period of time. In the Hindu tradition, due to the tropical climatic conditions and due to the religious beliefs, the body of the deceased is disposed of as soon as possible.

Thus the absence of the deceased in his physical form is quite sudden, unexpected and difficult to accept. In many ways the vivid ceremonies, the repeated invocation of the preta and relating to it as if physically present, maintain a sense of proximity with the deceased. It allows the bereaved to come to terms with irreversible Physical absence of their loved, one over a period of time. Thereby the shock of the suddenness of death is buffered.

After having gone through several days of intense and unfamiliar ceremonies, the bereaved are ready to and also need to lessen the intensity of their feelings and expressions. By this time, they have been prepared to accept the reality of their loss for the most part. While the prescribed period is by no means indicative of an end to the grief, it gives the bereaved adequate strength, to ease back into their normal daily activities and life. They will eventually come to terms with their loss in the course of time.

The thirteenth day is a day of welcoming auspiciousness

śubhasveekaraṇaṃ for the family. The period of religious impurity being over, the family visits a temple to offers prayers to the Lord, in an environment of auspiciousness and religious purity. They resume their usual prayers at the family altar at home, by lighting a lamp. Purificatory prayers are performed, members of the family wear new clothes and invite their extended family and friends, who shared in their grief over the past few days.

All of them show their care and support for each other. The bereaved family makes use of this opportunity to express their gratitude to their extended family and friends, who stood by them during a very difficult period in their lives.

The essential prayer of the day is:

शिवं मे अस्तु सदा गृहे ।

śivaṃ me astu sadā gṛhe

May there always be auspiciousness in our home.

While religious tradition has established the duration of the ceremonies over a period of thirteen days, the scriptures also point out that time itself is experienced differently by different forms of life. In the Vedic tradition time has been understood as essentially not having an absolute reality. In fact, a person experiences time differently during waking, dream and deep sleep states. Thus the number of days experienced by individuals on earth is not experienced in the same manner by a Thus the absence of the deceased in his physical form is *pretā Pitṛ*, *deva* and so on. One does not know for certain, in terms of our concept of time when a *jīva* will assume another birth of a physical body. It is for this reason that when oblations are performed for ancestors, one invokes three generations of ancestors to represent all of them.

5

PROCESS OF BEREAVEMENT

The human mind being complex as it is goes through intense and at times overwhelming reactions during the process of bereavement. Bereavement is defined as a reaction to the loss of a loved one and separation from those upon whom one depends on for comfort, sustenance and sanctuary. Even in the animal kingdom,

it is striking to see the reaction of an animal to the death of one of the members of their family or group. For a moment or longer an animal will remain around the dead member as though perplexed at its lack of responsiveness, and the animal's behavior implies an uncertainty or confusion about what has happened. Sooner or later it appears to leave reluctantly and continue with its life.

A human being reacts to any loss with grief and mourning. Grief is a normal and a common human experience, as no one is spared from the experience of loss, or from events that cause sorrow in one's life.

Mourning is a process by which a person experiences and resolves his grief. Most people go through a series of normal feelings and reactions during their bereavement.

Upon losing a loved one, a person often goes through an initial state of shock and feelings of numbness or bewilderment. The person is in despair and may react with disbelief over what has happened, by thinking or acting as if the deceased person is still present. Thus the initial response may be one of denial or anger. His distress and suffering is evident in crying, sadness, loss of appetite and difficulty sleeping. It is not uncommon for the bereaved to feel guilty and blame themselves, for acts of commission or omission towards the deceased person.

There is a yearning for their presence, an inner restlessness and a preoccupation over the events leading to the person's death, or of the final days or the past. A human mind deals with any trauma, whether minor or major, by ruminating over it. This helps a person get over the traumatic experience. Death of a loved one is a major traumatic event in one's life, and it takes a length of time to adequately get over the trauma.

The circumstances of death also affect the bereavement process. When death is sudden and unexpected, the initial reaction of disbelief is intense. It is difficult for one's mind to accept the fact that a person, who was very much alive and part of one's world, is gone in an instant. The experience of losing a loved one abruptly makes the uncertainty of one's own life very evident, and one becomes very much aware of the ephemeral nature of one's own existence. The void felt within oneself is very deep.

When a person dies after a protracted bout of illness or after a prolonged age, and his death is anticipated, the bereaved usually have some time to adjust to their inevitable, impending loss. In such an instance, one's mind starts imagining what it would be like to lose the person, how one would manage their affairs and the feelings one might have. However, one is unable to truly anticipate what will happen until one actually lives through the experience. After numbness and disbelief, comes the feeling of anger. Anger is born out of helplessness. The bereaved may express anger by blaming others for the death of their loved one. They often blame the medical personnel who had been involved in the care of the deceased. They may also blame other family members for not doing enough. Some of this blame is due to their own guilt, at perhaps not doing all that they could have done, to save their loved one.

It is not uncommon to see misunderstandings between family members of the deceased. As each one attempts to deal with their own conflicting emotions, they take out their frustrations on one another. Sometimes people blame God, who is seen as having the ultimate responsibility for everything that happens in the universe. The average person understands God as someone who gives what one desires when prayed to. And, their experience tells them otherwise, because their God did not grant their wish for their loved one to survive. Thus, even a normally devout person may get angry and reject religious traditions that could have been of comfort to him.

Eventually the grieving process results in an acceptance of the reality, that is, the irretrievable loss of a loved one. One gets resigned to the reality of the loss, as one has no choice in the matter. Over a period of time the intensity of sadness lessens. One is able to participate in and enjoy pleasant things in life.

The void that is created by the absence of a loved one is filled by his memories. Sooner or later most people come to terms with their loss and are able to accept the reality that their loved one is gone from their life physically. Reconciliation of this loss permits them to continue with their own lives. To this end, they may identify with some of the characteristics of the person

they have lost, thereby gaining strength and security from the person they cherished. The acuteness of pain and sorrow diminishes and the person feels like returning to their normal life.

It is important and necessary for an individual to go through the process of bereavement. Only by doing so, one is able to overcome the trauma of one's loss, such that it allows one to continue with one's life in an emotionally healthy manner. Sometimes, one has difficulty acknowledging one's feelings because they are unpleasant and difficult to bear. In such instances one denies to oneself the reality of the emotions one experiences. Thus there is an inner contradiction in what one feels and what one allows oneself to experience. When one allows oneself to experience emotions that occur naturally in one's mind, and is able to acknowledge them to oneself, one is more in touch with one's nature and is able to grow from the experience, however unpleasant, difficult or painful it may be.

In current times, when families are scattered all over the world and separated by distance from their loved ones, one may have to deal with the death of a family member at a distance. Because of Hindu traditions, the initial ceremonies involving disposal of the body of the deceased, are performed immediately after death and one is not able to participate in it by one's physical presence. In these instances an individual may wonder whether it is necessary to travel the long distance since "everything is over". However, one need not minimize the importance of participating and being physically present for the remainder of the ceremonies during the grieving period. Being with one's bereaved family, sharing the common loss, expressing one's feelings to those who can relate to it intimately because of their relationship, are all important to the process of bereavement. Therefore, unless there is an unavoidable reason, it is advisable to physically participate in the ceremonies and be with one's family during the prescribed period of mourning.

A loved one who is deceased is always remembered. There is no such thing as "completely getting over" or "resolving" the death of a loved one. There are recurring occasions in one's life when the absence of a loved one is felt, with varying degrees of sadness. However, one is able to experience this feeling without much discomfort and continue to live happily.

There are rare occasions when a person is unable to overcome the grieving process. His sadness becomes more instead of less. He is incapacitated and unable to take care of himself fulfill his responsibilities. The passage of time does not seem to help and he becomes unable to function. When this happens, such a person may need extra help of a professional to help him overcome the intense reaction to the trauma.

6

ANTYEṢṬI SAMSKĀRA (LAST RITES)

INTRODUCTION

Every individual goes through a variety of life experiences and is called upon to deal with different situations. Some of the situations are more difficult to deal with than others. Among these, one, which is unavoidable, is to cope with the death of a person one is close to and one cares for. While everyone faces death some day, either one's own or another's, few are inclined to spend time thinking about its implications.

People in every society have developed customs and perform religious ceremonies to deal with the death of an individual. The traditions that they follow are meant for the well being of the deceased who is no more and the bereaved that remain. Hindu traditions connected to the death of an individual, have sustained through several thousand years.

They have sustained because they are profound in meaning, beneficial psychologically and sensitive to human emotions. When understood, their importance cannot be minimized.

Samskāra sacraments mark the important milestones in the life of a Hindu. The rites connected to the death of an individual, *Antyeṣṭi* is the final *Samskāra* in the life of an individual. As it is a sacrament, a family member closely related to the individual has the obligation and privilege, to perform these religious ceremonies.

Human beings dispose the body of their loved one with great respect and care. This is an expression of their reverential attitude towards life. The final rites are two-fold; ones that deal with proper disposal of the dead body of the deceased, and those that are performed during the thirteen days of mourning that follow the funeral ceremony.

Death implies an irretrievable loss of a person from one's life. It is especially traumatic to one's psyche when one is closely connected to the deceased. Following the death of a person one is close to, one goes through a period of intense initial reaction. The initial reaction is followed by a process of bereavement in order to get over the trauma. Religious ceremonies are of considerable help to a person during this process. Understanding the content and principles that underlie the customs and religious traditions, makes it meaningful for the one who follows them, and also for the ones who participate in the process.

In observing the *Antyeṣṭi Samskāra* of a Hindu one finds some differences in customs among people from different regions of India.

While there may be some variations in cultural customs and expressions, the religious ceremonies are similar. However, they may be performed in a more or less elaborate manner by different groups of people. Needless to say, all the ceremonies are based on Vedic insights and traditions.

What follows in this section is a discussion on the essence of the various ceremonies during the immediate period after death, including the funeral ceremonies and the ceremonies performed during the prescribed period of mourning.

Antyeṣṭi or *Antima* ***Samskāra***

A *Samskāra* is defined in Sanskrit as: *Samyak kriyate yena karmaṇā iti samskāraḥ* which means final or *Antima*. A ***Samskāra*** is a religious action by which one is sanctified and made a qualified recipient for performing a particular religious activity or for gaining a desirable result. or oblation. Thus ***Antyeṣṭi Samskāra*** is the final ritual or oblation in the lifetime of a Hindu.

Bodhāyana Pitṛmedhāsūkta (3.1.4) states:

जातसंस्कारेण लोकमभिजायति मृतसंस्कारेण अमुं लोकम् ।

jātasaṃskāreṇa lokamabhijāyati mṛtasaṃskāreṇa amuṃ lokam

*By the sacrament jātakarma (**Samskāra** performed after birth) one gains desirable ends in this world, by the sacrament performed upon death one gains a desirable world hereafter.*

The individual responsible for and expected to perform the final sacrament on behalf of the deceased is his son (eldest, if there is more than one). If the deceased was bereft of a son, then his grandson (born of his daughter), or a male relative connected to him in the patrilineal line such as his brother or brother's son, or a relative belonging to the same gotra (*sagotram*), or connected to him patrilineally (*sapiṇḍam*) has the privilege of performing the ceremonies.

This custom is not because of bias against daughters but is a reflection of the patriarchal nature of most of Hindu society. Additionally, it reflects the customary manner by which most rituals are performed, which is that a man performs the ritual with the consent and participation of his wife and other women in the family. A deceased person's wife can also perform the ceremonies directly, or with a priest as proxy. If there is no relative, his teacher (*ācārya*), student (*śiṣya*) or even a friend (*suhṛd*) are qualified to do so. According to Hindu scripture, for one who has no relatives or friends, the king (the state, in current times) is obligated to perform the necessary religious ceremonies.

Thus we see that while there is a definite order of priority in who performs the religious ceremonies, there are a lot of options provided in the tradition to address various possible scenarios. Having lived a spiritual life, it is only befitting that the final disposal of the dead body of the departed be done with sanctity, reverence and care.

The final ceremonies are described in the *Taittireeya āraṇyaka* portion of *kṛṣṇa yajur veda*. There are more detailed and systematic descriptions of these ceremonies in the *gṛhyasūtras* of *Bodhāyana* , *Bharadwāja*

Āśvalāyana and *Hiraṇyakeshee*. The *Garuḍapuraṇa* also describes in detail the ceremonies to be performed upon the death of an individual, including disposal of the body, rituals during the period of mourning and thereafter, and what happens to the jiva after his death. The jiva ,the indweller of the body is believed to survive death of it's physical body and continue it's journey of experiences. The physical body, which is made up of gross elements, is in itself lifeless and left behind by the jiva, who moves on. Through the history of humans there have been a variety of ways in which people have disposed of the dead bodies of their kind. It is of historical interest to note that with respect to Hindu customs there appears to be no evidence of disposal of the dead body by exposure (as in the case of Native Americans or Parsis) or by mummification (as among the Egyptians, who believed that the spirit remained with the dead body which therefore had to be preserved). Burial (in earth and water) is a recognized means of disposal in special instances as with respect to children below two years and renunciates,

Sannyasis

The method of disposal is in keeping with the Hindu belief of the continuity of journey of the j¢va after the death of its physical body. The body is, in it's essential nature, understood as being inert, made up only of elements and is a part of the physical world. From early Vedic times, that go back thousands of years, cremation is the most recognized form of disposal of the dead body among Hindus. The body is ritually offered back to the elements from which it originated. Cremation is much more than a consignment of an individual's corpse into fire for disposal. It is a religious act that involves prayer, invocation and sanctification.

Agni devata, the presiding deity of fire is invoked. He is looked upon as the carrier of oblations to the gods. Therefore, in rituals, a fire is lit in which Lord Agni is invoked and oblations, including the body, are offered. The ceremonies that are performed upon the death of a person are also called *ūrdhvadaihikakriyā* obsequies connected to the jiva.

The initial ceremonies are mainly expiatory rituals, *Prāyaścitta* karmas, and rituals meant to sanctify the body before it is offered unto the fire. A person who is aware of his imminent death, may wish to perform *Prāyaścitta* karmas himself before his death. He does this by performing a ritual called *kṛṣṇacaraṇam*. He performs *kṛṣṇacaraṇam* by taking a purificatory bath, *snānam*, and giving charity, *dānam*. Alternatively, he can just give *dānam* if he is not in a position to take a purificatory bath.

Ten types of objects such as cow, land sesame seeds, gold, money and so on, may be given away in *dānam* depending on one's affordability. If a person does not perform this ritual, his family, in order to atone for his unbecoming acts of omission and commission, namely *pāpakarma* and to help the jiva proceed in its travel, gives *dānam* on his behalf. The ten items considered appropriate for *dānam* are described in *Garuḍapurāṇa* a in the following verse:

गोभूमितिलहिरण्याज्यवसोधान्यगुडास्था ।
रजतं लवणं चैव दानानि दश वै विदुः ॥

gobhūmitilahiraṇyājyavasodhānyaguḍāstathā
rajataṃ lavaṇaṃ caiva dānāni daśa vai viduḥ

Cow, land, sesame seeds, gold, ghee, clothes, grain, jaggery, silver and salt are the ten types of d¡nam, *giving.*

7

CREMATION CEREMONIES

When a person is deceased, his dead body is to be cremated as soon as possible. When death occurs during the day, the body is usually cremated on the same day. When it occurs at night, it is cremated before the end of the subsequent day. Cremation is not performed during the night. People are sometimes constrained to keep the body of the deceased for a day or two, due to unusual circumstance. This may happen if they have to wait for a significant family member to arrive from a distance, or if they live in a foreign land. Even if a body has to be preserved for a period, it is not subjected to the process of embalming. Embalming would not be consistent with the process of ritual purification of the body for the purpose of cremation. If the body has to be preserved for a while it may be done in cold temperature.

While there may be regional differences in some of the customs, most rituals are quite similar in form and content.

Irrespective of the community or region one is from, a Hindu follows religious ceremonies based on the Vedas.

The ceremonies for the disposal of the body and during the subsequent period of mourning, are described elaborately in some of the hyms of the Vedas, *Gṛhyasūtras*, and *Dharmaśāstra*. Other traditional literature entitled *Antyeṣṭi paddhati*, and *Antyeṣṭi prayoga* also elaborates upon what is required to be done at this time.

Before cremation, the body is anointed with reverence and care. The ritual by which the body is anointed is called *abhiṣiñcanam*. It involves bathing or sprinkling the body with water for religious purification. While anointing the body, mantras are recited invoking sacred rivers in the water, calling upon them to purify the body, in order to make it qualified to be an offering unto Lord Agni. Sandal paste, *candanam*, vermillon powder, *kumkum*, sacred ashes, *vibhūti*, are applied on the forehead and the body is covered with new cloth and fresh flowers. A few drops of *gaṅgā* water and holy basil leaf *tulasi*, are placed in the mouth. After being thus prepared, the body is placed and anchored on a wooden frame made of bamboo sticks and laid with its head facing the south. Traditionally, the southern direction is looked upon as indicating mortality and death.

***Karṇamantra*:** Mantras are chanted in the right ear of the deceased, symbolically reminding the departed *jīva* that an individuals life span, the life breath, *prāṇa*, senses, mind, organs of action, earth, the universe and the Lord, are all interconnected. The idea in this message is that a jiva is not an isolated entity in the creation, but has been an integral part of an infinite universe, and continues to be so even after death of the physical body.

Pretāgnisandhānam: A ritual fire is kindled in which the infinite Lord is invoked as Agni *devatā*, presiding deity of fire. Depending on the status of the deceased person, for instance, whether married or a *brahmacāri*, male, female, a parent, child, adult and so on, various prayers and mantras are recited to invoke the Lord in the fire. In case of one who maintained a ritual fire, that is he performed *agnihotra* ritual daily throughout his married life, a ritual fire is kindled by taking an ember from the *agnihotra* fire. For such an individual, a final *agnihotra* ritual is also performed at this time.

Prāyaścitta Karma: This specific karma is called *gṛhyāgnilopaprāyaścitta*, a ritual of atonement performed by giving *dānam*, charity. It is performed if the death occurred at a time considered inauspicious astrologically. *Prāyaścitta Karmas* are also performed if the death itself occurred in a manner considered inauspicious such as an unnatural death, death of a mother following childbirth and so on.

After the above initial ceremonies are completed, the family and friends carry the body of the deceased in a procession, to the cremation site. The bier is carried on the shoulders of four members of the family and friends.

The eldest son, who generally performs all the rituals, leads the procession and is followed by the rest of the family and friends. In Vedic times women were encouraged to join the funeral procession. This practice was later discontinued. In modern times, we sometimes observe ladies accompanying the funeral procession.

The one who leads the procession carries in a clay pot, the ritual fire that has been kindled by the domestic fire which had been maintained by the departed during his lifetime. It is befitting that the person who maintained the *agnihotra* fire throughout his married life, in order to perform daily karmas, be cremated from the same sacred fire. Cremation itself is regarded as the final ritual in the life of an individual. In current times, since most people do not maintain *agnihotra* fire, the fire which is ritualistically kindled and in which Agni *devatā*, in invoked and prayed to is carried for the cremation ceremony. During the procession the participants chant *yamasūkta* from the yajur *veda* or chant the Lord's name, such as *jai śri Rām*, *Rām nām Sat hai* and so on.

Ekoddiṣṭaśrāddha: This is a *śrāddha* done invoking the departed. It is defined thus: *ekaṃ uddiśya yacchrādhaṃ ekoddiśya tad ucyate*, meaning *śrāddha* by which one individual is invoked. The purpose of this ritual is to make the body *dahanayogyaḥ*, qualified to be an offering, to Lord Agni invoked in the funeral pyre. Any offering that is made to the Lord undergoes a religious purification. Since the body is looked upon as an offering unto Agni *devatā* made ritually, it has to be made thus qualified.

Pañcapiṇḍadānam: Offerings are made to various presiding deities, *devatās* and ancestors, *pitṛs*. These are done five times, to seek the blessings of various deities and thereby remove obstacles in the jiva's journey. They are done by offering *piṇḍam* (rice ball offering),

1) at the site where death occurred, *mṛtasthānam*, to the *vāstu devatā* of the house,

2) at the doorway, *dvāram*, to the *dvārastha gṛha devatā*, presiding deity of the doorway,

3) during the procession at the crossroad or site of rest, *viśrāmasthānam*, to the *bhutayonis* and *devatas* to remove obstacles to the birth of the next form namely *preta*.

4) at the site of cremation to sanctify the ground and pyre and

5) at the time of collection of the ashes and remains, *astisañcayanam*

***Dahanasaṃskāraḥ*, Lighting the Pyre Ceremony:**
In the Hindu tradition, cremation of the dead body is not looked upon as merely a means of disposal of the corpse. It is looked upon as returning the body to the elements from which it was born. Furthermore, the dead body is symbolically offered back to the infinite Lord *Iśvara*, who is non-separate from the manifest universe. Returning the body is accomplished by offering the body unto *Agni devatā*, presiding deity of fire, who is ritually invoked in the funeral pyre.

***Sthalaśuddhi*:** The site where the body is to be cremated is sanctified by means of mantras and sprinkling water. The body is also sanctified by mantras and placed on a freshly prepared wooden pyre. *Agni devatā* invoked in the pyre in his specific manifestation as *Kṛvyadāgni*.

Ghee, clarified butter is offered unto the pyre that is then lit by the eldest son. Before lighting the pyre upon which the body of the deceased is placed the son goes around it three times chanting the following mantra:

कृत्वा तु पुष्करं कर्म जानत वाप्यजानतम् ।
मृत्युः कालवशं प्राप्य नरं पञ्चत्वमागतम् ॥
धर्माधर्म समायुक्तं लोभमोहसमावृतं ।
देहेऽयं सर्वगोत्राणि दिव्यान् लोकान् स गच्छतु ॥

kṛtvā tu puṣkaraṃ karma jānata vāpyajānatam
mṛtyuḥ kālavaśaṃ prāpya naraṃ pañcatvamāgataṃ
dharmādharma samāyuktaṃ lobhamohasamāvṛtaṃ
deheyaṃ sarvagotraṇi divyān lokān sa gacchatu

Having performed known and unknown actions for attaining prosperity, having gained timely death and resolved the physical body into the five elements, having concluded a life of desires and connected to Dharma *and* Adharma*, may you proceed to heavenly realm.*

Again, while the pyre and body is in flames the departed is addressed in the following manner:

प्रेहि प्रेहि पतिभिः पूर्वेभिः यात्रा नः पूर्वे पितरः परे यः ।
सङ्गच्छस्व पितृभिः संयमेन इष्टापूर्तेन परमे व्योमन्

prehi prehi pathibhiḥ purvebhiḥ yātrā naḥ purve pitaraḥ pare yaḥ
saṅgacchara pitṛbhiḥ saṃyemena iṣṭāpurtena parame vyoman

The deceased in the form of preta *is implored to go forth, leaving behind all pāpas on the ancient path on which our ancestors have gone.*

While being implored thus, clarified butter, *ghee*, black sesame seeds, tilam, and water are offered unto him.

Prayers also implore *Agni devatā* (*Oṃ kṛvyadāya namastubhyam* and so on) to lead the jiva to the heavens as indicated in the following verse:

अस्मात्त्वमधिजातोऽसि त्वदयं जायतां पुनः असौ स्वर्गाय लोकाय स्वाहा ।
त्वं भूतकृद् जगद्योनिः त्वं लोकपरिपालकः अपसंहर तस्मात्त्वं स्वर्गं नय मृतम् ॥

asmāttvam adhijātosi tvadayaṃ jāyatāṃ punaḥ
asau svargāya lokāya svāhā
tvam bhūtakṛdjagadyoniḥ tvaṃ lokaparipālakaḥ
apasamhara tasmāttavaṃ svargaṃ naya mṛtam

You are born of this (fire) and you sustain it (as its presiding deity). You are the repository and the protector of all beings.
Take unto you the deceased one and lead him to heavenly abode.

Additionally, prayers also implore that, may the eyes proceed to *Sūrya devatā* may *prāṇa* proceed, to *Vāyu devatā*, May you (the jiva) proceed to the realm of experience, *lokaḥ*, that is beneficial to you according to your *puṇya* and so on.

Thus, all the organs that constitute the body are offered back unto the elements from which they originated, and the family and friends bid farewell to the departed with prayers for his future welfare.

In current times, the body may be cremated in an electric crematorium. While this is acceptable, all religious aspects of the ceremonies are still observed.
After the cremation ceremony is over, the family and friends return from the cremation grounds. Before they return to their homes, they have to take a purificatory bath. They do this with their clothes on, as the clothes also are to be washed as a part of the religious custom of observing *maḍi*, religious purity. The family members of the deceased (*bandhūs*) offer oblations of water, *udaka tarpaṇam*, to the deceased while facing south, and offer prayers to *Prajāpati*.

After this they sit for a while talking about the departed and about the transient nature of life and the world. They then return home. Before entering the house they place the right foot on a steppingstone reciting the mantra:

अश्मनिव स्थिरो भूयासम् ।

Aśmaniva sthirō bhūyāsam

May we remain steadfast as this stone.

Asthisañcayanam: This ceremony is connected to the collection of the ashes and other remains from the site of cremation and their final disposal. In early Vedic times the females in the family performed the collection of the ashes and remains. In current times the person who lit the pyre goes along with some family members and collects the ashes. This ceremony is performed on the first, third, seventh or ninth day following cremation. In this regard Dharma¿¡stra mandates the following:

प्रथमे अह्नि तृतीये वा सप्तमे नवमे तथा ।
अस्तिसञ्चयनं कार्यं दिने तद्गोत्रजैः सह ।।

prathame ahni tṛtīye vā saptame navame tathā
asthisañchayanaṃ kāryaṃ dine tadgotrajaiḥ saha

On the first, third, seventh or ninth day collection of the ashes and remains is to be performed along with relatives belonging to one's gotra.

The pile of ashes and remains is separated and anointed by sprinkling milk on it while chanting mantras. A homa, fire ritual is also performed. Prayers to the departed implore him or her to assume another form. The ashes and remains are then immersed in a body of water. The place of immersion is generally a sacred river such as ***Gaṅgā*** or the ocean. Hindus place considerable faith in the purifying strength of sacred rivers and, it is a common custom to carry the ashes to a site of pilgrimage such as *Gayā*, *Prayag*, *Varaṇasī* and so on to immerse the ashes of a family member.

The following verse indicates the sanctity accorded to the above custom:

गङ्गातोये च यस्यास्थि प्लवते शुभकर्मणः

न तस्य पुनरावृत्तिः ब्रह्मलोकात् कदाचन ।

गङ्गातोये च यस्यास्थि नीत्वा संक्षिप्यते नरैः

युगानां तु सहस्राणि तस्य स्वर्गे भवेद्गतिः ॥

gaṅgātoye ca yasyāsthi plavate śubha karmaṇaḥ
na tasya punarāvṛttiḥ brahmalokāt kadācana
gaṅgātoye ca yasyāsthi nītvā samkṣhipyate naraiḥ
yugānām tu sahasraṇi tasya svarge bhaved gatiḥ

For the one whose ashes and remains are immersed in the Ganges, following auspicious ceremonies, there is no return from the heavenly abode. He remains there for thousands of yugas.

After the funeral ceremonies and cremation are completed the family returns home and observe a period of mourning. During this time other religious ceremonies are performed and family and friends visit them to offer their condolences.

8

CEREMONIES DURING MOURNING PERIOD

Religious Impurity (*aśaucam*):

In the Hindu tradition the period of mourning is generally observed for thirteen days. Hindus also observe religious impurity *aśaucam*, during this period. It is important to understand the practice of *śaucam*. religious purity, and its corollary *aśaucam*, religious impurity, because these practices are highly misunderstood by the average person.

Religious impurity is a form of religious practice that is observed in most religious traditions. For example, in the Jewish tradition there is a concept of Kosher, whereby food is considered religiously pure or impure, depending on certain criteria established by the Jewish tradition. Among the orthodox they "keep kosher" by maintaining a kitchen and cooking according to strict rules of sanctity. They also follow other religious rules by observing Sabbath and so on. In Islam, the holy site of Mecca is accessible only to people of Islamic faith and the presence of one who is not a Muslim is seen as a defilement of it's sanctity and is not acceptable. Certain protocols with respect to attire are mandated, to be able to enter the Vatican. In the Zorastrian tradition only people belonging to that tradition can enter their house of worship. Thus we see that people all over observe various customs that establish criteria by tradition, whereby they maintain certain kinds of religious purity, in regard to their religious practices.

It is important to note that in the Hindu and some other religious traditions this practice in no way implies that a person is labeled as pure or impure by the religious tradition. Among Hindus, *śaucam* is commonly practiced with respect to all forms of worship and prayers, in order to maintain sanctity of the religious forms. Thus, one is required to purify oneself by a bath before performing worship. One also sanctifies articles of worship, by anointing them with holy water and chanting specific mantras prior to their use.

During the period of bereavement the immediate family of the deceased observes *aśaucam* or religious impurity with respect totheir regular daily worship or going to the temple. During this period, all the ceremonies performed by them are in connection with the departed.

Death while natural and inevitable, is looked upon as an inauspicious occurrence as it brings sadness and grief to all affected by it.

The period of observance of *aśaucam* varies,depending on several factors such as, the age of the person who Is dead, one's relationship with the departed and one's community traditions. For example, if the person who died was below two years of age then *aśaucam* applies only to the child's parents for one to three days.

If the individual happens to die before undergoing the *samskāra* of *nāmakaraṇam*, naming ceremony there is no period of *aśaucam*, beyond the age of upanayana *samskāra* it is observed for the full period prescribed.

In case of Brahmins who are routinely engaged in religious activity the prescribed period of observing mourning is ten days. Here again, among them, the one's who maintain *agnihotra* and study Vedas daily observe *aśaucam* for only one day as they are required to do their agnihotra ritual daily. Those engaged only in study of the Vedas observe *aśaucam* for three days and others for ten days. Those of other communities like *kṣatriyas*, *vaiśyas* and *śudras* observe *aśaucam* for ten, fifteen and thirty days by virtue of the professions and the kind of religious activities they engage in. It is optional for friends and distant relatives to observe *aśaucam*. Friends observe *aśaucam* by taking a purificatory bath upon returning to their homes after the funeral ceremony, or after a visit to the house of the deceased during the prescribed period of mourning. The bereavement of various people is, determined by their relationship with the deceased.

During the period of *aśaucam* one is required to refrain from performing *pūjā* and during the grieving period one is expected to follow appropriate behavior indicating sorrow and grief.

First Day Ceremony:

The *jīva* during it's life was very closely associated and

identified with a particular body. It was also connected and attached to other individuals, such as his family and friends. Due to this close identification with it's body that is no more, it is believed that a *jīva* could have some difficulty proceeding on it's onward journey.

Before it takes another birth, depending on i's karmas, it continues it's experience in the form of, and subsequently assumes another body. As a transitory state, after it has relinquished his physical earthly body and before assuming the form of *pitṛ* it assumes the body called *pretaśarīraḥ*. Just as in the case of a human birth it takes nine months for a child to be fully formed, it is believed that the *pretaśarīraḥ* is fully formed in nine days. The rituals that are performed for these nine days are for the well being of the *jīva* who is in the form of ***preta***.

During the ceremonies, the presence of the ***preta*** is invoked on an icon, *piṇḍa*, by a ritual called *pāśānasthāpanam* and offerings are made of water and black sesame seeds by a ritual called *vāsodakatarpaṇam* and *tilatarpaṇam*. The *tarpaṇam* (offering of water and black sesame seeds) is performed daily up to the 10th day, or, they may all be done at one time on the 9th or 10th day.

Asthisañcayanam: This ceremony involves the collection of the ashes and other remains and is performed by the family members of the deceased. During the ritual the remains are sprinkled with milk and water and mantras are chanted. A fire ritual, *homa*, is performed invoking *Agni devatā*

Rituals in the form of *prāyaścitta karmas* are performed. Offerings are made to the departed. Prayers are performed to the departed to assume another form to continue his onward journey.

Asthivisarjanam: After the fire ritual, the ashes and remains are immersed in a body of water, where they disperse immediately to become one with the elements. Generally this is done in a river or the ocean. Many Hindus immerse ashes in one of the sacred rivers such as *Gaṅgā*, *Godāvari*, *Narmadā*, and *Kāveri*

Second to Tenth Days:

Aurdhvadehikasaṃskāraḥ: These rituals performed for the next nine days during which offering of rice ball, *piṇḍadānam*, is made to the departed. Just as a fetus takes nine months to develop, it is believed that the departed assumes a transient, intangible body *vāyavya śarīra*, called *preta*. This body is also called *piṇḍaja*, born of (in connection with) *piṇḍa*.

Tarpaṇam: This is a ritual in which offerings are made in the form of water, *udakatarpaṇam* and black sesame seeds, *tilatarpaṇam*. While the orthodox may do the rituals daily, they may alternatively be performed together on the 9th or 10th day. In some communities and some instances *aṣaucam* is observed for three days. Here again the ten *piṇḍas* are offered in the period of three days instead of ten days and a ceremony called *Nārāyaṇabali* is performed on the third or fourth day.

Tenth Day Rituals:

There are significant ceremonies performed on the tenth day among most Hindu communities. It is believed that on the tenth day the jiva has fully assumed the *Pretaśarīra* .

Prabhūtabali: Like a child at birth is hungry and needs food intake, the preta is believed to experience hunger and thirst and is offered significant amounts of food in the form of an offering called ***Prabhūtabali***. Special food items, which were particularly liked by the departed person, are prepared. The food that has been thus offered is then immersed in a river or ocean where it is consumed by other forms of aquatic life. In some communities the food is offered to birds, such as crow (*Kākabali*) or an animal like cow (*paśubali*). Prayers are offered to *Yama devatā* to facilitate the onward journey of the jiva.

Ānandahomam* and *Śāntihomam: Fire rituals are performed in order for the *jīva* to gain happiness and peace. The prayers on this day are also meant for the family to gain peace and tranquility in dealing with their loss. The ceremony includes paring of the hair, nails and beard of the survivors who perform the rituals. Some may shave their head as an expression of their bereavement.

Eleventh Day:

Several important ceremonies are performed on the eleventh day. These include offerings to the ancestors, *pitṛs*, *śrāddha*, giving gifts to the needy, *dānam*, and offering food to Brahmins, *brāhmaṇabhojanam*.

The rituals are purificatory and for *prāyaścittam*, atonement for the departed and well being of the family.

***Vṛṣotsargaḥ* or *Ṛṣabhadānam*:** Cattle in the form of a bull is given as *dānam* to a temple. *Brahmaṇas* are offered food and given *dakṣiṇā* in the form of a variety of useful gifts

Lord *Viṣṇu* is prayed to for the salvation of the *preta* with the following verse:

अनादिनिधनो देव शङ्खचक्रगदाधर ।
अक्षय्य पुण्डरीकाक्ष प्रेतमोक्षप्रदो भव ॥

anādinidhano deva śaṅkacakragadādhara
akṣayya puṇdarīkākṣa pretamokṣaprado bhava

O Lord, who are changeless and without beginning, holding a conch, discuss and mace in your hands, please grant this preta *freedom.*

Twelfth Day:

On the twelfth day there are important ceremonies performed. It is the last day of the immediate mourning period following thedemise of a person.

Sapiṇḍīkaraṇam **or** ***Ekoddhiṣṭaśrāddha*:** On this day the *jīva* is believed to give up its transitory *pretaśarīra* and assume theform of *pitṛṣarīra*. This is symbolized in the ritual in which four or six *piṇḍas* balls of rice are made; three for ancestors, *pitṛs* and one (or three) in which the *jīva* is invoked and offerings are made.

Following this, the *piṇḍas* representing the *jīva* are joined with the three representing the *pitṛs* symbolizing the union of *jīva* with its ancestors.

***Brāhmaṇabhojanam*:** Three *brāhmaṇas* are invited. In them one invokes the lord, the departed *jīva* and *pitṛ* and they are ritualistically given food.

Thirteenth Day:

This is the concluding day of the mourning period. It is a day in which purificatory rituals are performed. Prayers are also performed for, peace, *śānti* of the family members. *Śivam me astu sadā Gṛhe*, May there always be peace in our home, is the prayer of this day. The lord is invoked in the form of the nine planetary deities and prayers are performed (*navagraha pūjā*).

The family members wear new clothes, go to a temple, light a lamp at the altar at home and resume their daily worship. On this day it is believed that the jiva continues on his onward journey to the abode of *Yama devata*, the presiding deity of death.

9

CEREMONIES AFTER THE THIRTEEN DAYS MOURNING PERIOD

After the bereavement period of thirteen days there continue to be some ceremonies performed for one year. These are called *śrāddha ceremonies*. They are performed after one month, *Ūnamāsikaśrāddha*; after six months, *ūnaṣaṇmāsikaśrāddha* and after one year, *ūnābdhikaśrāddha*. The ceremonies are to be performed on the anniversary of the day of death, as calculated by the Hindu calendar based on the lunar cycle. Thus, they are performed on the *mṛtatithi*, lunar day anniversary of the relevant month. Sometimes all of them may be performed at one time at the end of one year.

The family continues to observe customs consistent with bereavement for the period of a year, in a less intense manner. The immediate family of the deceased, such as the spouse, male children and grandchildren avoid performing any major religious functions such as marriage. They also do not celebrate festivals that call for gaiety and display of fun and pleasure. They maintain a relatively low profile in social get-togethers.

10

ŚHRADDHA CEREMONY

Śhrādha is a religious ceremony that involves invoking and propitiating one's forefathers. The following verse in *Brahmapuraṇa* explains the important elements of a typical *śhrāddha*:

देशे काले च पात्रे च श्रद्धाया विधिना च यत्
पितृनुद्धिश्य विप्रेभ्यः यः दत्तं श्राद्धमुच्यते ।।

deśe kāle ca pātre ca śraddhayā vidhinā ca yat pitṝnuddiśya viprebhyaḥ dattaṃ śrāddhamucyate

śhrāddha is (a karma*) in which ancestors are invoked at the proper time and place, propitiated as prescribed and dakṣiṇā given to brahmaṇas.*

śhraddha means acceptance based on trust and reason.

śhrāddha is to be performed in keeping with religious tradition. It is performed at the appropriate time and place by one who is qualified to do so. It involves invoking and propitiating one's ancestors, inviting *brāhmaṇās* and offering them food and *dakṣiṇā*.

Certain times are considered auspicious for performing *śhrāddha* karma such as, *amāvāsya*, new moon day, *aṣṭaka*, the *aṣṭami*, eighth day of the lunar cycle of *kṛṣṇa pakṣa*, dark fortnight, of *hemanta*, and *śiśira ṛtu*s, autumn and winter seasons, during *saṅkrānti*, movement of the sun into the northern and southern solistices, and on *vṛddhikāla*, auspicious times such as marriage and birth of progeny.

śhrāddha is not identical to ancestor-worship of ancient cultures such as Egyptians, Babylonians, and Chinese. In cultures. Where there is ancestor worship, usually people believe that the ancestors remain for eternity and they are worshipped, much the same as gods and deceased saints are worshipped. While it is true that ancestors are invoked in *śhrāddha* ceremony there is a significant difference. Hindus accept the principle of karma and rebirth. Thus, they do not look upon as their ancestors as waiting in some place for eternity, who they can join and be with, after their own death.

śhrāddha ceremony is looked upon as a karma that is expected to have a result that benefits both its performer and the recipient. As those living in the earthly realm do not know with certainty, the timeframe in which beings in other states of experience operate, three generations are invoked as representing the ancestors. The prayer of a Hindu is always for his ancestors to move on with their experiences and journey that leads to freedom from the cycle of birth and death, and not wait around so that they can join them in the hereafter.

Additionally, *śhrāddha* is looked upon as an obligatory duty to be performed, to fulfill one's debt to one's ancestors, for all that they have handed down to us.

There are different types of *śhrāddha* that are described. Some of the commonly performed ones are described below.

Pārvaṇa śhrāddha:

This *śhrāddha* is defined as follows:

देशे काले च पात्रे च श्रद्धया विधिना च यत् ।
पितॄनुद्दिश्य विप्रेभ्यः यः दत्तं श्राद्धमुच्यते ॥

deśe kāle ca pātre ca śraddhayā vidhinā ca yat
pitṝnuddiśya viprebhyaḥ dattaṃ śrāddhamucyate

Pārvaṇa shrāddha is that in which three generations of ancestors, (along with their spouses) are invoked and propitiated.

Three generations of one's ancestors namely, father, grandfather and great grandfather are invoked. Their deceased spouses are also invoked and propitiated. In this *śhrāddha* five *brāhmaṇās* are invited.

In this connection tradition defines a *brāhmaṇā* as *bhojanadānayogyaḥ*, one who is qualified to be a recipient of food offering and *dānam*, gift of giving. The requisite qualifications include a thorough knowledge of the scripture as well as a thorough understanding of its meaning. Additionally such a person is not expected to be one who has given up following a life of religious discipline, that is *ācārabhraṣṭaḥ*.

In the ceremony, three *brāhmaṇās* called by the term *viśvadevapātrāḥ*, recipients of the deities *viśvadevas* occupy the place representing the *devas*. Two *brāhmaṇās* called *pitṛpātrāḥ*, recipients representing ancestors occupy the place of one's ancestors. The five of them are treated with honor and offered food. They are also given *dakṣiṇā* and their blessings are sought. The one who performs the ceremony ends it by seeking the following blessing:

दातारो नोऽभिवर्धन्तां वेदाः शान्तिरेव च ।
श्रद्धा च नो मा व्यागमद् बहु देय नो अस्तु ॥

dātāro no abhivardhantāṃ vedāḥ śāntireva ca
śraddhā ca no mā vyāgamad bahu deya no astu

O forefathers, may there be increase in knowledge and progeny for us. May there not be a decline in ¿raddha, faith based in trust, may there be prosperity for us.

Hiraṇya śhrāddha:

This is a simpler form of the above ceremony. It has fewer steps and it is performed when an individual is unable to perform the more elaborate version, for want of time or resources. In *Hiraṇya śhrāddha*, there is no fire ritual, and an elaborate meal is not prepared for the *brāhmaṇās*. Also *piṇḍa* offerings are not made to the ancestors.
This less elaborate ritual includes invoking and propitaiating ancestors by making offerings of rice and tilam, seeking their blessings and giving *dakṣiṇā*to the *brāhmaṇās*. Sometimes several *brāhmaṇās* may not be available. Such a *śrāddha* done is called *apātrkaśrāddha*. In this case *Devās* and three generations of ancestors are invoked in an icon made of a particular kind of grass used for rituals called *kūrcā*. Offerings of rice grains *taṇḍulam*, sandal paste, *candanam*, and holy basil leaves, *tulasi*, are made to *devās*. Offerings of black sesame seeds, *tilam* and water *udakam*, are made to ancestors. *dakṣiṇā* is also given to a Brahmin who may or may not be present during the ceremony. The person performing the *śhrāddha* ceremony also observes some form of religious discipline such as fasting, *upavāsa*, until the religious ceremony is completed and avoids intake of staple such as rice on that day. The day is also spent in remembering the departed, in praying to them and seeking their blessings for the well being of oneself and one's family.

Amāvāsya Tarpaṇam:

Tarpaṇam is defined in Sanskrit as follows:

तृप्यन्ति पितरो येन तत् तर्पणम् ।

tṛpyanti pitaro yena tat tarpaṇam

That (ritual) by which the ancestors are satiated is called Tarpaṇam

The ritual of *Amāvāsya Tarpaṇam* is performed every month on the new moon day. On this day a person who has lost one or both parent invokes them with two more generations of ancestors who are deceased. He performs oblations with water and black sesame seeds. He prays to them and seeks their blessings for the well being of himself and his family. He gives *dakṣiṇā* to a priest according to his capacity as a part of the ritual.

Nāndi śhrāddha:

This ceremony is called by many other names such as *Nāndimukha śhrāddha*, *Māṅgalika śhrāddha*, *Vṛddhi śhrāddha*, and *Ābhyudāyika śhrāddha*. It is performed on auspicious occasions such as marriage, *vivāha*, sacred thread investure, *upanayanam*, and birth of progeny, *jātakarma*. The purpose is to remember one's ancestors in recognition of one's indebtedness to them and pray for their blessings on the happy occasion. On this occasion *viṣvadevās* in the form of Vasu and Satya are invoked, along with ones ancestors, for propitiation and blessing.

Tīrtha śhrāddha:

This is the *śhrāddha* ceremony performed at a site of pilgrimage.

It is considered auspicious to perform *śhrāddha* at a site of pilgrimage such as *Gayā*, *Vārānasi*, *Kurukṣetra* and so on. These sites have sanctity associated with them that is based on history and religious tradition.

Jivacchrāddha:

This is a ceremony not commonly performed. It involves *antyeṣṭi karmas* performed by an individual for the sake of himself, while he is alive. A person may be bereft of progeny and family, or may be convinced that there is no one available to assume the responsibility, or feel an obligation, to perform his last rites after his demise. Thus, he would not have the benefit of the karma normally done to benefit the deceased. Since it is believed that karma inevitably leads to a result, the expectation is that one would nevertheless benefit from the results of the karma at a later time. Obviously, the intent here is not to indulge in a morbid fantasizing about oneself as dead and mourn for oneself.

The ceremony involves performing *śhrāddha* for ancestors, invoking and praying to the Lord in the form of various deities. The various deities invoked are: the presiding deity of Death and Dharma, *Yama devatā* and the presiding deity of cremation fire, *Agni devatā* in the form of the carrier of a deceased Jiva, *Kavyavāhanāgni*.

Yama devatā is also invoked in his many manifestations as *Dharmarājā*, presiding deity of Dharma as an order, *Mṛtyu* presiding deity of death,

Antaka, the one who terminates life, *Vaivasvata*, presiding deity of the current time, *Kāla*, presiding deity of time and *Sarvapraharaṇa*, one who draws everything unto himself.

Rudra devatā is invoked as the presiding deity of the cremationgrounds, *Śmaśānapati*..Once a person performs this ceremony, he continues to perform *śhrāddha* karma. A person generally performs *śhrāddha* karma for his own benefit

Generally this ceremony is performed only when death is immanent, and not when a person is young and in good health.

A persons connection with another person does not end upon the latter's death. This is especially so with regard to one's parent, grandparent, siblings and other significant people in one's life. Their influence on oneself can never be erased, nor is it necessary to do so. Parents continue to inspire, and bless us, and their memories continue to comfort us all our lives.

Vedic tradition recognizes one's indebtedness to one's ancestors. They are viewed with reverence and love. When one is able to appreciate the profoundness of their insight and the religious and cultural forms that they maintained, one cannot but be filled with gratitude towards them. They have often had to maintain our rich traditions, against hostile attempts to deprive them of their heritage and destroy their religious traditions and culture. In the Vedic tradition it is one of the obligatory duties of every individual to express their gratitude to their ancestors daily. One invokes one's ancestors, propitiates them and prays to them for their blessing. This is done by performing *ṛṣitarpaṇam* and *pitṛtarpaṇam*. In these ceremonies, water and sesame seed oblations are offered to ancestors who were seers *ṛṣis*, and one's immediate ancestors, *pitṛs*. *Śhrāddhakarma* done on specific occasions is another obligatory duty of a Hindu.

In acknowledging one's ancestors, one reaffirms one's roots. Every human being needs to have a sense of being rooted to their historical past, and their heritage. One's historical past forms an essential component of one's self-identity. Feeling proud of one's ancestry and heritage, and being grateful for being born in a culturally rich tradition, gives a sense of well-being and strength to one's character. One feels a part of an ancient culture and tradition, whose principles are truly universal and very profound. It is a tradition that encourages free thought and facilitates personal growth by a process of enquiry and teaching.

Unfortunately, one observes that some people do reject and turn away from their culture, traditions and religious upbringing. This is generally seen to be the result of an emotional reaction which is born of frustration, anger and resentment. It is sometimes a result of ignorance, erroneous thinking and lack of objective enquiry. When such a conversion occurs, the people involved do not merely express a preference in choice of religious tradition, but actively shun those that they have turned away from. Thereby, they shun a part of themselves.
That is the reason one finds such people overly critical, angry and even condescending towards others of their own original background.

They are ashamed of their own forefathers and what they stood for. Such a person, who sees himself as a product of a dysfunctional and primitive ancestry, will find it very difficult to have a healthy self-esteem, as he tries to dissociate with a past that he cannot deny is a part of him.

11

UNUSUAL CIRCUMSTANCES OF DEATH

Death may occur in a variety of circumstances that are considered to be unusual. The usual expectation is that a person who is born, lives a full average span of life. Additionally one expects that death, when it occurs, is because one's body has naturally declined to the extent that it is unable to function normally. Thus, when death occurs at a young age, by accident or intention, during pregnancy or childbirth, as an act of terrorism and so on, it is looked upon as a tragic inauspicious end to one's life. When death is inauspicious some additional rituals, in the form of *prāyaśccitakarma* are performed as a part of the ceremonies. Hindu religious tradition addresses how to deal with these circumstances.

Death of a Child:

Death of a child is an especially tragic event, certainly for the parents and immediate family, and also for others who are connected to them. One does not expect a child to die, as one does an older person. Therefore, the news of a child's death is especially shocking and unexpected. It is devastating for the parents, who have a lifetime of hopes and expectations for the new member of their family.
They feel cheated and victimized by fate and circumstance. When death occurs during infancy or in

utero, it seems a colossal waste of an individual's life. One naturally wonders what is the point to the jiva assuming a particular form if it was not meant to enjoy any life experience?

Explaining this tragedy with "it is God's will" or "God knows what is best" only makes God appear to be insensitive at best, or cruel at worst.

In trying to understand such an occurrence in terms of the karma model, one sees that while such a young child may not have had an opportunity to experience its own life, it certainly leaves a permanent impact on the lives of its parents and others connected to it. While it is impossible to understand all the implications of the laws of Karma, one can see that *jīva* that are connected to one another do affect each other by their presence, their lives and by their absence. Thus, such a birth does not seem to be totally without purpose.

In regards to the *antyeṣṭī* ceremonies with respect to children, for one who is less than two years old, the body of the deceased is not disposed of by cremation. Since cremation is a ritual, most of the ceremonies are not performed since a child is looked upon as being untouched by karma. Additionally the parents observe the practice of, religious impurity only for a period of one to three days. The body is disposed of by burial.

Stillbirth:

These are special circumstances where a developing fetus dies before it has taken birth. When the body is recoverable, then it may be disposed of in the same manner as in a very young child. That is, by burial without any of the specific ceremonies being performed.

Death Where the Body of the Deceased is not recovered:

Death sometimes occurs following tragedy when the body is not recovered. This might happen when there is an accident at sea, in a plane crash, as the result of an act of terrorism and so on. When this occurs, *antyeṣṭi* is still performed. The preta is addressed by facing in the direction in which the deceased was known to have departed. A symbolic representation of the deceased is created in the form of an effigy made out of a particular straw used for rituals, *kuśaputtali*. All final rites are then performed. The family observes the customary period of mourning.

Death of a *sannyāsī*:

The death of an individual who has taken to the order of a monastic life, *sannyāsī*, is treated as a special circumstance. Such a person is accorded the status of one who has overcome the cycle of birth and death, which is the goal of his spiritual pursuit. For him, as in the case of small children, no usual religious ceremonies are to be performed after disposal of the dead body.

The tradition observes the following rule:

त्रयाणामाश्रमाणां च कुर्याद्दाहादिकक्रियाः।
यतेः किञ्चिन्न कर्तव्यं न चान्येषां करोति सः ॥

trayāṇāṃ āśramāṇāṃ ca kuryād dāhādikakriyāḥ
yateḥ kiñcinna kartavyaṃ na cānyeṣām karoti saḥ

The last rites are to be performed for those belonging to the three āśramas (brahmacarya gṛhastha vānaprastha). The rites need not be performed for a ***sannyāsī*****:** *Neither does he perform them for another.*

When a person takes to the order of ***sannyāsa***, as a part of the ritual ceremony involved, he performs all his obligatory duties and rituals towards his ancestors in a final ceremony. After this final ceremony he is absolved from having to perform them again. Tradition frees him from all obligatory duties, in order that he may fully engage himself in spiritual pursuit. After death, his body is disposed of by burial. Sometimes, a venerated monk may have a monument built by those devoted to him. Other monks may honor his memory on the sixteenth day after his demise, by offering useful gifts to other ***sannyāsī****s* on his behalf.

12

VEDIC INSIGHTS

INTRODUCTION

The Vedas form a body of knowledge, upon which is based the way of life of a Hindu. Additionally, Vedic insights provide him the basis upon which he views life, himself and the world. The way of life based upon Vedic insights, is expressed in the social, cultural and religious traditions of a Hindu.

Just as a person seeks to find a meaning to life and living, he seeks a meaning in death, for death is an essential component of life. In fact, for a Hindu, life and death are not opposed and adversarial to each other. They are complimentary and exist together, much like the two sides of a coin. Together, they represent change, in as much as, the birth of an object implies death of its prior state, and its death implies the birth of its subsequent stage.

In order to understand the reasons that form the basis of the final religious ceremonies that are performed in connection with a person's death, it is necessary to know how a Hindu understands life and death. Birth and death are understood as being cyclical in nature. Birth of an individual from a state of nothingness, and culminating into an eternal existence is not consistent with Vedic insights.

Birth of a given form is understood as a manifestation of a sentient being, *jīva* in that particular form, and death as an event, that marks the *jīva* manifesting in another form. Thus, death as experienced by the living, does not mark the finish line of a single lifetime, but is a milestone in the onward journey of a *jīva*.
What follows in this section, is a discussion on Vedic insights that are relevant to the understanding of *antyeṣṭi saṃskāra* in the life of a Hindu.

SCIENTIFIC AND RELIGIOUS THOUGHT

In order to understand any phenomenon intelligently, it is important to understand the process of reasoning, by which an individual arrives at various conclusions, and gains knowledge that he considers acceptable. Both scientific and religious thought present us with models in order to understand the universe and the different phenomena that we experience.

Thus, one can understand a model as a logical system of thought, used to explain complex subjects meaningfully. For instance, there are many different medical models, developed to understand normal functioning and the disease process in the human body.

There is the allopathic model, the homeopathic model, ayurvedic model, and so on. Then again, there are models such as the genetic model that explains how a person is born with a given set of physical features, personality traits, cognitive capacities, susceptibility to illnesses and so on. Physical sciences have models that explain the physical laws by which objects function. For instance, Newtonian physics, Relativity, Quantum physics, atomic theory and so on. Psychology presents us with the developmental model, psychosexual model, interpersonal theories, behavioral model, family systems model and so on, to understand how the mind functions normally and abnormally.

Thus we see that science provides us with a means of knowing how things happen in the world. It does this by reducing the phenomenal world to its cause by observation through the five senses of perception. This method of knowing can be described as causative thinking. However, one can see that merely by knowing how things work, one is not able to appreciate the meaning behind what is happening.

To take an example, let us say a person wants to know how a watch serves its purpose, which is, to tell time. By knowing the laws of mechanics the person may be able to know how various components of a watch function, and how it tells time. However, this knowledge, which involves causative thinking, does not in itself help a person appreciate what is time, its importance, the value of punctuality, the reality of time as a concept and so on. Such an understanding requires a different kind or thinking that one might call purposive thought. Purposive thought is not based on observations by sense perceptions. It involves an abstract thinking process that includes insight, values, sensitivity and so on.

Thus, one can see that scientific models provide us with a basis to understand how various objects in the world and the universe itself functions. However, they do not intend to provide a means for an individual to find a deeper meaning with respect to life itself. It is a universal experience that a human being seeks to know something deeper about life and its purpose. Besides survival, seeking comfort and satisfying one's intellectual curiosity about the world one lives in, one seems to have an inner urge to discover something more profound and fulfilling about life itself and one's very being. One is unable to rest content by merely living, growing and procreating, as do other forms of life. One's quest seeks a deeper fulfillment. Religious thought addresses issues that are not available for observation by the senses, provide a person with a deep sense of purpose, and give profound meaning to one's life. Our religious culture and traditions help us in the fulfillment of the deep human quest.

13

THE LAW OF KARMA

The Vedic culture and tradition provides us with a karma model, in order to explain many fundamental questions connected to the life of a jiva. For instance, what determines the birth of an individual? Why is one person born rich and one poor; one a genius and another retarded, one in an environment full of opportunities and comfort while another is born in an environment of abuse and neglect, one born free and another oppressed? How is it that life sometimes appears to provide a series of opportunities to a person who frequently finds himself at the right place at the right time, while another seems to keep missing the bus and all of his efforts seem to be in vain?

Are these circumstances arbitrary and purposeless? Are they caused by a superpower that has a warped sense of humor and a peculiar sense of justice, or is there an order

in their occurrences that is purposeful and flawless? The karma model is based upon the principle of cause and effect. Just as, every action has a reaction, any action done by an individual is understood as invariably producing a result.

The action done by an individual is called karma and its result called *karmaphalam* (literally translated as fruit of action).

The type of action performed and one's effort determine the nature of the *karmaphalam*. When an action is performed, its result may be obtained immediately, for instance, in performing the action of walking one obtains the result of moving forward.

The result of an action may alternatively be achieved at a later period in time, as in case of planting and harvesting. The results that are perceived are called *dṛṣṭaphalam*, seen results. Thus with respect to action and its results there are two factors that are obviously operating namely effort, *prayatnam* and time, *kālam*.

There is another type of *karmaphalam* described in the scriptures called *adṛṣṭaphalam* or *adṛṣṭam*. In one's life experiences one finds that the results of one's actions do not seem to be determined solely by effort and time. There appear to be other unknown factors, which make the difference between the successful outcome and the failure of an action. This unknown factor is called *adṛṣṭam* (literally translated as unseen). The unseen factors are not arbitrary in case of a given jiva, but are a consequence of actions done by it in the past. Unlike other forms of life, a human being has been endowed with a capacity of making choices in terms of actions. He is not pre-programmed at birth as an animal is. Additionally, there is the presence if a moral order called Dharma that is inherent in the creation. Thus, in making his choices a person invariably ends up choosing actions that may conform to the universal Dharma or may be opposed to it.

Thus, in regards to action and its results, one can recognize the influence of a third factor which is unseen, *adṛṣṭam*. The third factor is also called d*aivam* which means divine. It is a factor that one is subject to and has to be accounted for. It is not created by any individual, and is not arbitrary, because no universally applicable law is seen to be arbitrary. In the case of a jiva, *adṛṣṭaphalam* operates as *puṇyapāpam*. Actions performed in keeping with dharma give unseen results called *puṇyam*, and actions performed against dharma result in unseen results called *pāpam*. It is the *puṇyam* and *pāpam* generated by prior actions done by a jiva that become the unknown contributing factors that determine the outcome of one's current situations.

14

KARMA, BIRTH AND REBIRTH

Any event is a caused happening. It is not an accident in the sense that it is not uncaused. In fact, any event that we call accident is only an incident whose causes are not fully known by us. The birth of a *jīva* is also looked upon by us as an event which has to have its own causes. Some of these are known and some unknown. Medical knowledge helps us understand how a jiva is born, in terms of the causes that are evident to us such as conception, development, viability of the fetus and so on. Genetic models reveal causes of some of the individual differences in ones cognitive capacities and susceptibility to illnesses. In regards to cause-effect connections one sees an orderliness and consistency, not chaos and randomness. While scientific models can help one understand how certain differences between individuals come about, they are not meant to address the question of why disparities between them occur.

How does one to find meaning in the fact that one *jīva* is born advantaged and one is not? What unknown factors cause one to be born in a cultured and comfortable home environment, and another in an underprivileged slum surrounded by crime and absence of values, education and culture?

For no apparent fault, what makes one person be subject to a series of misfortunes, sorrow and suffering while another appears to have good fortune showered upon him at every turn, and that too unasked?

Scientific enquiry is unable to answer these questions because they are outside its domain. Scientific enquiry deals with causative thinking not purposive thinking as described earlier.

Questions seeking a purpose to life fall under the purview of philosophy and religious thought. To answer such questions by saying that all differences are random occurrences and due to chance is to make human existence devoid of meaning and purpose. Moreover, if random occurrences are seen to be universal and widespread, they are no longer random but reveal orderliness. To answer questions related to human suffering by saying it is the just and mystical will of an unknowable God, who is a formless divine power residing in an unseen location, is to give the answer an ambiguity that a reasoning mind finds difficult to accept . Such an answer also contradicts one's concept of God as a compassionate, just and benevolent Being. To reduce one's questioning and one's attempts at reason to the status of a blasphemy, is to deprive a human mind of its natural desire to seek knowledge.

Generally scientific thought is considered to be rational, philosophy is looked upon as being speculative and theology as a belief system that is not available for verification and based on unquestioning faith. In regards to the Vedic tradition, one finds that religious thought, including its beliefs, is based on a process of enquiry, and is therefore open to questioning, rational, and not contradicted by one's experiences.

According to the karma model, whereas every action performed has a seen and an unseen result, the unseen *puṇya* and *pāpa*results when they fructify in time, become the determining factors for the disparities among various jivas at the time of thei birth.

In this regard, *puṇya* gives rise to factors that are conducive to desirable and favorable circumstances and *pāpa* gives rise to the opposite situation. Thus the actions performed in the past themselves become the cause for what is later experienced by it. Not only this, but also conformity to the universal values of Dharma and Adharma (right and wrong) also become relevant in case of a *jīva* such as a human being, who is endowed the faculty of choice in performing action.

In the world one finds that no existent thing seems to be subject to total annihilation. Both matter and energy always exist in one form or another. One never creates matter or energy from a non existent cause; one can only convert energy or matter from one form to another. Even the dissolution of the world mentioned in the Vedas refers only to an unmanifest condition of the world, like a tree in a seed. In addition to matter and energy, conscious beings also exist in the world. If matter and energy do not come to an end, why should a conscious being? The conscious being is known as *jīva*, *prāṇī*, or to use a western expression, the individual soul.

The end of matter-energy vestige called the live physical body need not bring termination to the conscious being. The scriptures confirm the supposition that the individual soul survives the death of the physical body, and continues to take on different bodies according to its past karmas, actions. Rebirth accounts for certain disparities among people which can perhaps be traced to their past individual karmas.

Para-psychologists have methodically documented cases of people who remember their past lives, further supporting the theory of rebirth.

The *Bhagavad Gītā* (2.22) says:

आ वासांसि जीर्णानि यथा विहाय नवानि गृह्णाति नरोऽपरानि
तथा शरीराणि विहाय जिर्नान्यन्यानि सम्याति नवानि देही ॥

vāsāṃsi jīrṇāni yathā vihāya navāni gṛhṇāti
narō'parāṇi
tathā śarīrāṇi vihāya jīrṇānyanyāni saṃyāti navāni dehī

Just as an individual discards the worn out clothes and takes on new ones, similarly jivas leave the worn out bodies and take on new bodies.

Types of Karma:

Sañcita Karma:

Over innumerable lives a given *jīva* performs countless actions, the results of which accrue to that particularr *jīva*. The total results of such karmas which have yet to fructify are called ***Sañcita***. Any karma which remains unfructified in this life, is credited with the other unfructified karmas in his account becoming a part of *sañcita Karma*.

From the pool of *Sañcita*, certain karmas called *Prārabdha Karma* precipitate a new birth, and are exhausted at the end of the current life of the *jīva*.
All results of actions that one performs do not manifest at one time. When a given set of karmas taken from the total pool of *Sañcita Karma* of a jiva fructifies, the jiva, in order to enjoy the results of these karmas, assumes a given form of life.

A *jīva's* birth is due to the pressure of karma which has to fructify. Without an appropriate body, time and place, the fructification of karma is not possible. Different sets of karma fructify in different births of the jiva. This process of karma exhaustion and accumulation continues until one gains *mokṣha*, freedom from birth and death.

Prārabdha Karma:

The particular set of karmas that fructify at any given time, thereby becoming the cause of the assumption of a particular form is called as *Prārabdha Karma*. *Prārabdha Karma* differ from one *jīva* to another bringing about differences between individual living beings. Additionally, they are responsible for the varying circumstances beyond one's control, favorable or otherwise, in an individual's life. Since the *Prārabdha* is a result of the fructification of both *puṇya* and *pāpa* every human being experiences both joy and sorrow in life.

Āgāmi karma:

Whenever a *jīva* gains a human birth or an equivalent to it elsewhere, he gathers new karma by use and abuse of free will. These new karmas, known as *Āgāmi karma*, accumulate in the jiva's ***Sañcita*** pool.

Thus all karmas performed produce results, karma-phalas which give rise to new births where one again performs karmas, which, in turn, create more karma-phalas. Thus, the *jīva* travels through births and deaths, trapped in the cyclic nature of karma.

In *Pañcadaśī* (1.30), it is said:

कुर्वते कर्म भोगाय कर्म कर्तुं च भुञ्जते ।
नद्यां कीट इवावर्त्तद् आवर्त्तान्तारमाशु ते ॥

kurvate karma bhogāya karma karttuṃ ca bhuñjate
nadyāṃ kīṭa ivāvarttād āvarttāntaramāśu te

They perform actions for experiencing their results and again they experience the results for performing actions. They go from birth to birth, as worms that have slipped into a river are drawn from one whirlpool to another helplessly.

The scriptures tell us that even the gain of heaven is only a result of good karmas and therefore limited to a given time period. When the *jīva*'s *puṇya* is exhausted, he will return to earth.

The *Bhagavad Gītā* says:

ते तं भुक्त्वा स्वर्गलोकं विशालम् क्षीणे पुण्ये मर्त्यलोकं विशन्ति

te taṃ bhuktvā svargalokaṃ viśālaṃ
kṣīṇe puṇye martyalokaṃ viśanti

Having enjoyed the multifarious heavenly pleasures they return to the world of mortals upon exhaustion of (their) puṇya karmas.

Puruṣārtha karma:

In observing the lives of various jivas one finds that in case of living beings such as animals, their life and actions seem to be totally predetermined.
They seem preprogrammed to act in a particular manner, without being able to make choices. Their life is spent in experiencing and responding to their environment as they are programmed to do. A human being on the other hand, is endowed with an additional capacity of deliberately choosing his actions. Within the parameters of his capacities there is a freedom of choice given to him. *Puruṣārtha karma* are actions done while exercising one's freedom of choice. The capacity of free will also plays a significant part in how a person modifies and is affected by his circumstances. While one can question the degree of free will as it is unknown, one cannot reasonably question its presence with respect to a human being.

Kāmya karma:

K¡mya karma is an action done based upon a desire for a particular end. Most of an individual's activity has its basis in *Kāmya karma*.

Prāyaścitta karma:

Prāyaścitta karma is an act of compensation performed by an individual, for another act that he performed in the past, knowingly or unknowingly which resulted in ***pāpa***, an undesired result of wrongful action. *Prāyaścitta* is not to be understood as a self-punitive action meant to alleviate guilt for transgressing a mandate. It is connected to the law of karma. Since it is in keeping with Dharma, *Prāyaścitta* karma performed gives rise to *puṇya*. This in turn contributes to reducing the unfavorable result of ***pāpa*** born of actions done in the past. *Prāyaścitta* is mainly in the form of *dānam*, sharing what one has with those that do not, specific prayers and *vṛatam*, specific religious vows.

Like the very creation itself, life and death for a *jīva* is looked upon as being cyclical, not linear. In other words, birth of a *jīva* is not the coming into being of an individual out of a non-existent nothingness, but the manifestation of that which was unmanifest prior to its birth in a given form. Thus, manifestation of a *jīva* in a given form is what constitutes it's birth. When this reasoning is extended beyond a single life it accounts for disparities in a *jīva* such as circumstances of birth, parentage and so on. It also provides a reasonable basis for the understanding of rebirth.

Jīva or *Prāṇī* and Life After Death

An individual sentient being is referred to by the name *Jīva* or *Prāṇī* in the Sanskrit language. The word *Jīva* is derived from the root *Jīv*, meaning to live. Thus, an individual living being is called *Jīva*. *c* is the life giving force that keeps a body alive, even though the body is by its essential nature inert. The word *prāṇa* can refer to the life giving breath and also to the intangible life principle abiding in an individual body.

A sentient being is conscious be it a human, an animal or a plant. Even a plant has life; hence it can die. While alive it grows, reproduces and responds to its environment. It survives in a favorable environment and when uprooted or deprived of its life sustaining nutrients, it dies. Animals are also living beings. In comparison with plants, animals are considered a more evolved form of life. Like plants they grow, reproduce and respond and to their environment. However, they are mobile and capable of more deliberate behavior. They can identify with their species and interact with other species. They are functionally and physically more complex than plants.

Among the three forms of life identified above, the human being is looked upon as the most evolved, as he is the most complex. He has an awareness of himself as a person, and an awareness of others as individuals. He has a mind, intellect, a free will and so on. He develops a fairly well defined self-identity and forms judgments about himself others.

Our scriptures confirm that the *jīva* or survives death of it's physical body. What is perceived and experienced as the phenomenon of death, is only a state of a given physical body. While a particular body ceases to be alive at one point in time, it's indweller continues to exist.

The *Bhagavad Gītā* (Chapter 2.12) Lord *Kṛṣṇa*, confirms the following:

न त्वेवाहं जातु नासं न त्वं नेमे जनाधिपाः ।
न चैव न भविष्यामः सर्वे वयमतः परम् ।।

na tvevāhaṃ jātu nāsaṃ na tvaṃ neme janādhipāḥ
na caiva na bhaviṣyāmaḥ sarve vayamataḥ param

Never, at any time have I been born, (nor have I) not existed. So also you and these rulers of me. Never shall we cease to be. We all shall continue to exist (after death of the physical body).

15

LIFE AFTER DEATH

According to the model presented in the Vedic tradition, an individual is made up of gross, subtle and causal bodies. These are described as follows:The gross body, called *sthūla śarīra* in Sanskrit, is made up of the tangible physical or anatomical body. It functions along with the physiological systems called *prāṇa* that keep it alive. Besides the gross tangible body one has a mind, intellect, memories and so on, which are not tangible.

These are said to constitute the subtle body or *sūkṣma śarīra*. Whereas the gross body can be perceived and objectified by the sense organs, the subtle body is not available for sense perception. However, the subtle body can be objectified cognitively to an extent, as when one observes one's thoughts, feelings and memories. One experiences the physical world during the waking state of experience, by means of the gross and subtle bodies. One experiences an inner subjective world by the subtle body, while totally preoccupied with thought or while in the dream state.

Besides the gross and subtle bodies, there is what is called the *kāraṇa śarīra* or the causal body that is not available for objectification, but which is in the form of the potential cause with respect to an individual.

To understand *kāraṇa śarīra* one can look at the example of the deep sleep state, where, from the standpoint of a jiva's experience, both the gross and subtle bodies have become unmanifest and are not available for experience, and they become manifest again upon waking up. While unavailable, the gross and subtle bodies do not disappear but remain potential in a causal form, as far as the individuals experience is concerned.

Similarly for a *jīva* the total unmanifest *Sañcita karmas* constitute the potential which become the cause for its births. The manifest *Prārabdha karmas* become the cause for its particular birth.

At the time of a *jīva*'s death, the *prāṇa*, physiological system, stops functioning in its given physical body. The constituents that make up the gross body undergo a transformation, by returning to their elemental form. The *jīva*, minus the particular gross and subtle bodies assumes another form according to its karmas. In a subsequent manifestation, a *jīva* may assume a form that is made up of gross and subtle bodies that are more or less exalted than a human form, depending on the preponderance of *puṇya* or *pāpa* karmas, that have fructified from the *Sañcita karmas* accrued to that jiva.

The cycle of birth and death continues until a *jīva* frees itself by gaining what in the Vedic tradition is called *mokṣha* or liberation.

Pretaśarīra:

The vedic tradition describes an intermediary state of being for a jiva immediately after its death. During this period the deceased is referred to as preta. In order to live a complete life of experiences in this world a jiva needs to totally identify with its particular individuality.
In this process it forms relationships and attachments to people and possessions. Death as an event does not abruptly terminate attachments as it does the existence of a given physical body. The jiva is believed to take a while to separate itself from its prior identifications, before being free to continue its subsequent experiences.

Certainly, the bereaved also require time to adapt to the reality of their abrupt loss. The period of thirteen days made up of religious ceremonies and social bereavement customs, are meant to be sensitive to the needs of the bereaved and the needs of *jīva*, as revealed by the Hindu scriptures. The scriptures reveal that after death of its physical body, the jiva experiences for a while the results of its karma, in the form of pleasant and unpleasant experiences. The realms of experience are called *lokās* of which there are several. When it has exhausted the results of a particular set of karmas and when more karmas fructify it is again born in the earthly realm.

The ceremonies that are performed during the cremation and the period of mourning encourage the jiva to move on. The prayers and rituals performed by the family benefit the *jīva* by encouraging it to continue in its journey. They also help the bereaved with the process of bereavement. After the twelfth day following its death the deceased is no longer referred to as preta.

He is believed to have joined the ranks of ancestors *pitṛs*. At a time unknown to us the *jīva* manifests in another form of life to continue its karma based experiences.

16

ĪŚVARA

To fully appreciate the law of Karma one needs to understand it in the broader context of *Īśvara*, the Lord and Dharma, the universal moral order as taught in the Vedic tradition. The law of Karma is related to an individual, his actions and the results of his actions. However, it is not merely a mechanical law like the Newton's law of action and reaction. Relevant to understanding the Law of Karma, it is necessary to take into account the one who is the giver of the law. The law of Karma, along with all the other laws in the universe, is a part of a purposeful order.

In understanding how any purposeful object like a watch or a pot comes into being, we find that there are two types of causes necessary. One is an intelligent cause, called *nimittakāraṇam* and the second, a material cause called *upadānakāraṇam*. In the intelligent cause resides the knowledge of the object to be created. Thus, in the example of a pot, there is the pot maker who is the intelligent cause and there is clay that is the material cause from which the pot is made.

Upon analysis of various objects in the universe, it is evident that everything in the universe seems to have a definite and meaningful purpose.

In short, what one observes is a definite order in the universe, where nothing happens without a purpose. Being purposeful its coming into being must necessarily involve preexisting knowledge. The locus of knowledge with regard to the infinite universe is what we understand as *Īśvara*.

Īśvara is thus understood as the all-knowing intelligent cause of the universe that we experience. One now has to account for the material cause. The universe is known to be infinite. Time and space are also considered to be a part of it. Therefore, one cannot look upon the material cause of the infinite universe as separate in time and space from the intelligent cause. *Īśvara* is thus understood as both the intelligent and material cause of the entire universe including time and space.

Is it conceivable for both causes to exist upon the same locus? A well-known example of such an occurrence is the dream. A dreamer experiences a dream world, including dream objects, pleasant and unpleasant situations, emotions, time, space and even himself. It is the dreamer who creates the dream out of his own unconscious memories born of prior experiences. In other words, the dreamer draws from his memories the material of his dream. The dreamer is thus the intelligent cause and also the material cause from which the objects of the dream world come to manifest and are experienced.

If one were to ask, where in the dream world is the dreamer located, the only reasonable answer would be all over, the dream world not being apart from the dreamer. In conclusion, we would encounter a situation in which the material and the intelligent cause are not separated from each other in time and space and abide in the same locus.

In a similar manner, when we understand that *Īśvara* is both the intelligent and material cause of the entire universe one can understand how the universe does not exist apart from the *Īśvara*. The law of Karma, being a part of the manifest universe that is experienced by us also is non separate from *Īśvara*, the Lord. Vedas confirm this by the statement in *Īśāvāsyopaniṣad*

ईशावास्यमिदं सर्वम् ।

Īśāvāsyamidam sarvam

Īśvara pervades all this (entire universe of names and forms).

17

DHARMA, THE UNIVERSAL MORAL ORDER

The Vedic tradition understands *Īśvara* as both the intelligence and the material cause of the universe. In its vision there is nothing that is apart from *Īśvara*. All the laws in the universe, including the law of karma and the law of dharma, are understood as the manifest expressions of *Īśvara*. Dharma can be understood as the universal moral order or in other words, the order involving right and wrong. Dharma is a Sanskrit word derived from the root *Dhṛ* that means to sustain. Dharma sustains jiva, the individual, through the cycle of birth and death.

A human being is subject to Dharma. Among living beings, we observe that only a human has a capacity of making deliberate choices. All other animals are born with predetermined behavior patterns. For instance, whereas an animal does not have the capacity to choose its diet, a human can choose to be a vegetarian or otherwise.

Obviously, this choice is not absolute, in that there is no choice in having the capacity to choose and one's capacity to choose may be influenced by some predetermined factors. However, it is the capacities for deliberate thinking and choosing, to whatever degree it is available, which makes a human being unique in the world that we know.

A human is also endowed with a basis, upon which he can make his choices. For instance, he may make them based on his desires. However, since he is not alone in the world and there are others too endowed with the same capacity, if his choices are based purely on desires they may very well conflict with desires of others, thereby disturbing the harmony between them. The laws in the universe always tend to support harmony and order.

Choices that are based on preserving universal harmony, and preventing conflict within oneself and between oneself and others, are based on universal values. An example of such a universal value is truthfulness. Another example is, not hurting others by word or deed. Without being taught by anyone, everyone senses these universal values. They are understood as part of the universal moral order, Dharma. Actions that conform to the universal values, thereby preserving harmony and preventing conflict are "right" actions, and those that go against the universal values, may be called "wrongful" actions. Right actions result in an unseen result, *adṛṣṭam* called *puṇya* leading to situations favorable to one's pursuits, and wrong actions lead to the unseen result called ***pāpa*** that leads to situations unfavorable to one's pursuits.

When a person lives a life primarily on the basis of conformity with Dharma, that is, the universal moral order, he gathers favorable results *dṛṣtam*, seen and *adṛṣtam*, unseen.

He enjoys the seen results in this life. He enjoys the unseen at a later time either in the current or a later life. A person can, by his choice live in a manner that goes against the principles of Dharma. When this happens, the unseen results of his actions accrue to him in the form of

pāpa that are unfavorable consequences to be experienced in his current life or later. Thus, we see how Dharma is applicable to a human being, since he is endowed with free will and the capacity to choose the course of his actions. Dharma, does not apply to animals. That is the reason why we do not attribute "right and wrong" to animals. In fact, we even absolve very young children from the responsibility of right and wrong, until they reach an age of understanding and have the ability to exercise free will.

The Vedic tradition emphasizes that an individual does not escape from the consequences of actions performed by him. A particular birth is only a manifestation of j¢va in it's current form, and death, its manifesting again in another form. The cycle of birth and death always remains within the scope of the universal order including the order of Dharma and the laws of Karma. Dharma the universal moral order is thus understood as an expression of the infallible order that is *Īśvara*, the Lord. The law of Karma is with respect to action and its result. When one takes into account the factor of right and wrong, dharma and adharma in Sanskrit, the law of Dharma is akin to the law of Karma. Being an expression of the infallible, the laws are not prejudicial, biased or arbitrary.

By appreciating this fact, one develops a reason based trust in the order, that is, in *Īśvara*. The trust in the infallible, that is *Īśvara*, frees oneself from the sense of feeling victimized or deprived.
Taking responsibility for ones actions, and at the same time having trust in the *Īśvara*, makes one mature in dealing with both life and death.

In the Hindu tradition, *Īśvara*, the Lord is invoked as *Yama devatā*, the presiding deity of death. *Yama devatā*is also looked upon as the presiding deity of Dharma.

Thus, *Yama devatā* is invoked and propitiated during the funeral ceremonies. Death is therefore not a frightening evil thing, but the counterpart of life itself. Life and death go together as two sides of a coin. In fact both of them together represent change, and one does not exist without the other. It is said that a wise person appreciates the similarity between the two.

आ जातस्य वै मनुष्यस्य ध्रुवं मरणमिति विजानीयात्
तस्मात् जाते न प्रहृश्येन्मृते च न विषीदेत् ।
अकस्मादागतं भूतं अकस्मादेव गच्छति
तस्माद् जातं मृतं चैव संपष्यन्ति सुचेतसः ॥

jātasya vai manuṣyasya dhruvaṃ maraṇamiti vijānīyāt
tasmāt jāte na prahṛṣyenmṛte ca na viṣīdet
akasmādāgataṃ bhūtaṃ akasmādeva gacchati
tasmād jātaṃ mṛtaṃ caiva sampaśyanti sucetasaḥ

Knowing that death is indeed certain for one who is born, do not be overjoyed at birth and morose upon death. Unexpected, a person is born, and suddenly he goes. Therefore, the wise perceive birth and death evenly.

18

UNDERSTANDING *MOKṢA*

Most religious traditions have a concept of the ultimate goal of a human life as reaching a place after death, located somewhere unseen, and staying there permanently. The place is enticingly described as being very desirable and called by various terms such as, heaven, paradise, *svarga*, and so on. Depending on their faith, different religious traditions also establish certain requirements for entry into that place. The requirements are generally of the nature of unquestioning acceptance of the tenets of that particular faith. A fearful and undesirable place is also described, as a punitive place, where people who do not accept the tenets of a given faith are permanently assigned.

Vedas also describe *lokās*, various fields of experience, wherein a *jīva* undergoes desirable and undesirable experiences which are the results of its own karma.

However, the Vedas also explain that since limited actions in themselves give limited results, no field of experience is permanent. Additionally, every experience by its very nature begins and ends which is what makes it an experience.

A verse in the *Bhagavad Gītā (9.21) reiterates:*

ते तं भुक्त्वा स्वर्गलोकं विशालम् क्षीणे पुण्ये मर्त्यलोकं विशन्ति

te taṃ bhuktvā svargalokaṃ viśālaṃ
kṣīṇe puṇye martyalokaṃ viśanti

Having enjoyed the vast realm of happiness, when the puṇya isexhausted, they return to the world of mortals.

A *jīva* thus moves from one field of experience to another. In this process, it assumes various forms. Some of these forms are called *bhogaśarīra*, where it mainly experiences the results of prior actions without generating new results of new karmas. Other forms, where a j¢va has the faculty of choice allow it to experience the results of prior actions and also perform new actions within the context of dharma, universal moral order.

These choice based actions result is *adṛṣtam*, unseen results in the form of *puṇya* and ***pāpa*** which then becomes the cause for subsequent births. Thus the cycle of birth and death, based on karma and its results, continues for a given individual *jīva*. This cycle is called *saṃsāracakra*, the wheel of *saṃsāra*.

In the Vedic tradition the ultimate goal for a human being is understood as becoming free from the In the Vedic tradition the ultimate goal for a human being is understood as becoming free from the In the Vedic tradition the ultimate goal for a human being is understood as becoming free from the *saṃsāracakra*, wheel of *saṃsāra* Freedom from a life of becoming, of change and limitation is called *mokṣa* a. The word *mokṣa* is derived from the root muc, meaning to be free, wheel of *saṃsāra*. Freedom from a life of becoming, of change and limitation is called *mokṣa*. The word *mokṣa* is derived from the root muc, meaning to be free, wheel of *saṃsāra*. Freedom from a life of becoming, of change and limitation is called *mokṣa*. The word *mokṣa* is derived from the root *muc*, meaning to be free.

The gain of *mokṣa* is called *mukti*. *Mokṣa* is not a recommendation, prescription, advice or offer by the scripture or an individual, but is naturally sought after by every human being. While a person may not be able to identify this goal as described, it is a universal experience that one seeks to be free from a life of limitations. It is a universal experience that no human being accepts being limited in terms of knowledge, happiness, mortality and so on.

Everyone seeks to be rid of the feeling of limitation and seeks to be full and complete within oneself. This fundamental universal quest, to be at home with oneself is based on one's experience of oneself as limited and incomplete. The Vedas explain that, if being limited was one's essential nature, then one would not seek to be rid of it, and one would be comfortable with it.

One would not want to reject that which is in keeping with one's essential nature much the same as one does not want to stop breathing that is natural. In fact, one gets very disturbed when there is any hindrance to the breathing process. The implication here is that being limited is foreign to one's essential nature.

A question naturally arises here that if being limited is foreign to one's essential nature, what causes one experience oneself as a limited person. The experience of oneself as limited also is universal and verified by one's conclusions about oneself. The only possible way to understand this seeming contradiction is that one is ignorant of the truth about oneself. Since everyone starts by being ignorant of the world, including oneself, one is not expected to know oneself as being free from all limitations. Additionally, one's self identity and the conclusions one reaches about oneself are all based on factors external to oneself, such as one's sense perceptions, opinions of others and so on. So, it is unavoidable that one sees oneself as being limited and lacking in many different ways.

By a process of enquiry and insight, the Vedas guide one to recognize one's essential nature as being free from limitations. Once this self recognition takes place, one does not mistake oneself as an isolated individual entity, an insignificant speck in the vast infinite universe, helpless and limited in every way. One gains intimate knowledge of oneself as the one infinite consciousness on which everything else has its being. One sees no separation between one's essential self and everything else.

Much the same as a wave stops seeing itself as a limited and isolated entity, different from other waves and the ocean, when it recognizes its essential nature as water. In this ultimate self-recognition, the jiva recognizes the falsehood of its individuality. Since all the karmas are performed by the jiva, with self-knowledge they get nullified, and the jiva gets freed from all the effects of previous and new karmas.

Since this knowledge is about oneself its truth can be ascertained within one's lifetime. One who has gained self-knowledge as described is called a *jīvanmuktaḥ*, liberated in life. With respect to the remainder of his life, a *jīvanmuktaḥ* continues to live with knowledge of his fullness, free from any sense of limitation and complete within himself. With respect to subsequent lives, he is freed from the cycle of birth and death, since the karmas which cause new births are nullified with self knowledge.

Until one gains self-knowledge which gives *mokṣa*, one is subject to the laws of karma and its results and all the rules of the universe are relevant and applicable, as also the ceremonies explained in this book.

Even though the Vedas discuss rebirth and heavenly experiences, its commitment is not to establish rebirth or an experience in heaven, as the final goal of a jiva. By revealing the jiva's rebirth, the Vedas only point out that one cannot get away with improper actions, and conversely, one will not be unrewarded for proper actions. Further, the connection between one's karma and *adṛṣṭam*, namely *puṇya* and *pāpa*, reveals a law which is known as the law of karma. Thus, one always reaps the results of one's actions, if not now, then later. Keeping this in mind, the Vedas want the individual to exercise prudence in his or her choice of actions.

19

JÌVANMUKTI

Vedas classify all human pursuits into four common ends, known as *puruṣārthas*: *dharma*, ethics; *artha*, securities; *kāma*, pleasures; and *mokṣa*, liberation. While the pursuits of security and pleasure are more or less common to all living beings, *dharma* and *mokṣa* are unique to human beings.

Artha, being the foremost urge in every individual, should necessarily be the first in the order of *puruṣārthas*. But in the tradition, *dharma* is given the first place because of its importance in choosing the means of gaining both *artha* as well as *kāma*. *Kāma* also is a *puruṣārtha* in as much as mere survival is not enough for a human being; every person alive wants to be happy. Insecurity and unhappiness are not mere psychological traits. They are much more basic, being centered on the core person. Neither the physical body, nor the mind has any sense of insecurity or unhappiness. It is the self-conscious person, manifesting in the sense of 'I', who feels insecure and unhappy.

Therefore, the basic problem of the human being is the sense that 'I am insecure', 'I am unhappy'. There is no solution to this problem of insecurity and unhappiness through the fulfillment of desires. No matter how long or how often I create favorable situations, replete with desirable objects and persons, the basic problem will never be adequately addressed.

It is a common experience that the insecure and the unhappy person continues to remain the same no matter how many times he or she tries to be otherwise. This process of becoming is called *saṃsāra* in the Vedic language. Freedom from this struggle to acquire and become is called *mokṣa*. Essentially, everyone is struggling to gain *mokṣa* even though he or she may not have recognized this pursuit underlying all other pursuits in life. The solution to this basic problem can only be in the form of self-knowledge wherein I recognize that "I am already free from insecurity and unhappiness". Such an understanding is not the end product of any becoming process. Either I am already free from being insecure, unhappy and limited, or I am bound forever.

Self Knowledge

If I am already free, I have to know myself. In the Vedic vision, the self is free. The Vedic tradition holds a body of knowledge, which leads one to recognize the nature of oneself as full and complete. That is the reason why in this tradition the ultimate goal of life is not called salvation, but freedom, *mokṣa*.

Mokṣa is the already existent the nature of one's self which is not produced, *utpādya*; not reached in time or place, *āpya*; brought about by a process of changing or modification of a previous state, *vikārya*; or brought about by a process of purification, *saṁskārya.*

An action, karma, whether religious or worldly, can produce only the four types of results just mentioned. Being the subject of all actions, the self is not a product of any of these four types of results.

The self, being already self existent, is self evident that is, not dependent on another for it to become evident. The sense of bondage which is centred on oneself, is due to ignorance and error. Thus self-knowledge is *mokṣa*, which is gained only by knowing the self as free from any form of limitation. Any knowledge is as true as its object because it is not subject to choice. An apple is an apple. One does not have the option of taking it as an orange. Knowledge of the self is no exception to this rule. It is as true as the self.

The *Upaniṣads* reveal that the self is limitless and methodically lead one to the discovery of this fact. The ignorance of the self is therefore the source of a life characterized by the pursuit of security and countless other ends. Thus, the whole pursuit of *mokṣa* is reduced to the pursuit of self-knowledge. And the one who has come to know the self to be free is a free person. Such a person is called a *jīvanmuktaḥ* and his or her state of freedom is called *jīvanmukti*, freedom from all forms of limitation here and now.

A Heavenly Belief

Anything less than *jīvanmukti* which is available here and now implies a promise of heaven later, after death.

A religion that offers such a promise is rightly called a faith, in as much as, one has to believe and live and die with it, in order to reach heaven.
Therefore, there will always be a number of people who will not believe in such a non-verifiable promise. That there is a heaven is a belief. That one will reach heaven after death is another belief. That one will like heaven after gaining it is yet another belief. That one will not come back is an unbelievable belief. Just as anything that begins must one day end, so too, a heavenly life that begins must necessarily come to an end. Also, a *mokṣa* that is dependent on a series of beliefs in the hereafter cannot be a solution to one's life fraught with afflictions here and now.

The *Upaniṣads*

The part of the Vedas which deals with the basic problem of the human being is called *mokṣaśāstra*. It is also called *Vedānta* because this part of the teaching is found at the end of each Veda. The teaching itself is in the form of teacher-student dialogues called the *Upaniṣads*. By exposing oneself to this body of knowledge through a traditional, one gains *mokṣa*, the knowledge of oneself. There are many statements in the *śāstra*, scriptures indicating *mokṣa* as being in the form of knowledge.

In one of the *Upaniṣads* it is said:

jñānāt muktim avāpnuyāt

may one gain freedom through knowledge.

The *Bhagavad Gītā*, which has the same subject matter as the *Upaniṣads*, also says:

jñānaṃ labdhvā parām śāntiṃ nacireṇādhigacchati

one gains lasting peace the moment one gains self-knowledge.

In his commentaries on the *Upaniṣads* and the *Gītā*, *Ādi Śankarācārya* helps us clearly see that one has to know the free self as unfolded by the *Upaniṣads* in order to be free.

The Role of Karma

Karma, in the form of prayers and rituals, constitute a religious and spiritual life. If knowledge is the means for *mokṣa*, what role does *karma* play in one's life? Does the performance of such actions have any relevance in the pursuit of *mokṣa*? *Karma* plays an important role in preparing a person for this knowledge. No one can circumvent the necessary preparedness for self knowledge, as even one cannot celebrate one's sixty-first birthday unless one has already celebrated one's sixtieth birthday. The maturity that can be gained by living in conformity with dharma and a prayerful life, cannot be gained in any other way. But what can be gained by knowledge cannot be gained by any prayer or *karma*. Therefore, the position of karma in the pursuit of *mokṣa* is very elaborately discussed in the *Upaniṣads* and the *Gītā*, and commented upon in detail by *Ādi Śankarācārya*.

The Vedas do talk about heaven and its desirability. By one's good *karma* one is promised a heaven, *svarga*. But the Vedas also reveal that heaven, like anything else in this world, is time bound and being the finite result of a finite action one will lose it in time.

The Ultimate End

One who has gained self-knowledge is a *jīvanmuktaḥ*, liberated while living. Such a person becomes a teacher for others who seek this knowledge. Knowing the self which is free from doership and enjoyership, he is free from all his past *karma*. No future *karma* can be accrued, for the same reason that he does not see himself as a doer or an enjoyer. As long as the set of *karmas* which has brought the current body into being lasts, he lives the life of a *jīvanmuktaḥ*. At the exhaustion of this *karma*, the body falls away and there is no longer an individual soul separate from *Īśvara*, the Lord.

Jīvanmukti is thus the ultimate end of every individual's life. The Vedas do not merely point out the end but also provide a way of life to discover it, giving a direction and a purpose to one's life. In order to gain its ultimate vision, *mokṣa*, it is essential to understand every aspect of the Vedic religious culture.

25919262R00067

Made in the USA
Lexington, KY
14 September 2013